I0494657

# SUNSHINE COAST
## *Endless Memories*

Sunshine Coast is a metropolitan area and the third most populated area in the Australian state of Queensland. Located 100 km north of the state capital Brisbane in South East Queensland on the Pacific Ocean coastline, its urban area spans approximately 60 kilometres of coastline and hinterland from Pelican Waters to Tewantin. The estimated urban population of Sunshine Coast as at June 2014 was 297,380, making it the 9th most populated in the country.

The area was first settled by Europeans in the 19th Century with development progressing slowly until tourism became an important industry. The area has several coastal hubs at Caloundra, Kawana Waters, Maroochydore and Noosa Heads. Nambour and Maleny have developed as primary commercial centres for the Hinterland.

AUTHOR: SOLÉ PAEZ
PHOTOGRAPHER: SOLÉ PAEZ

*This work is copyright. Apart from any use permitted under the Copyright Act 1968, no part may be reproduced by any process, nor may any other exclusive right be exercised, without the permission of Solé Paez (Photographer) and Ximena Varas (Illustrator).*

COVER & INTERIOR DESIGN: SOLÉ PAEZ

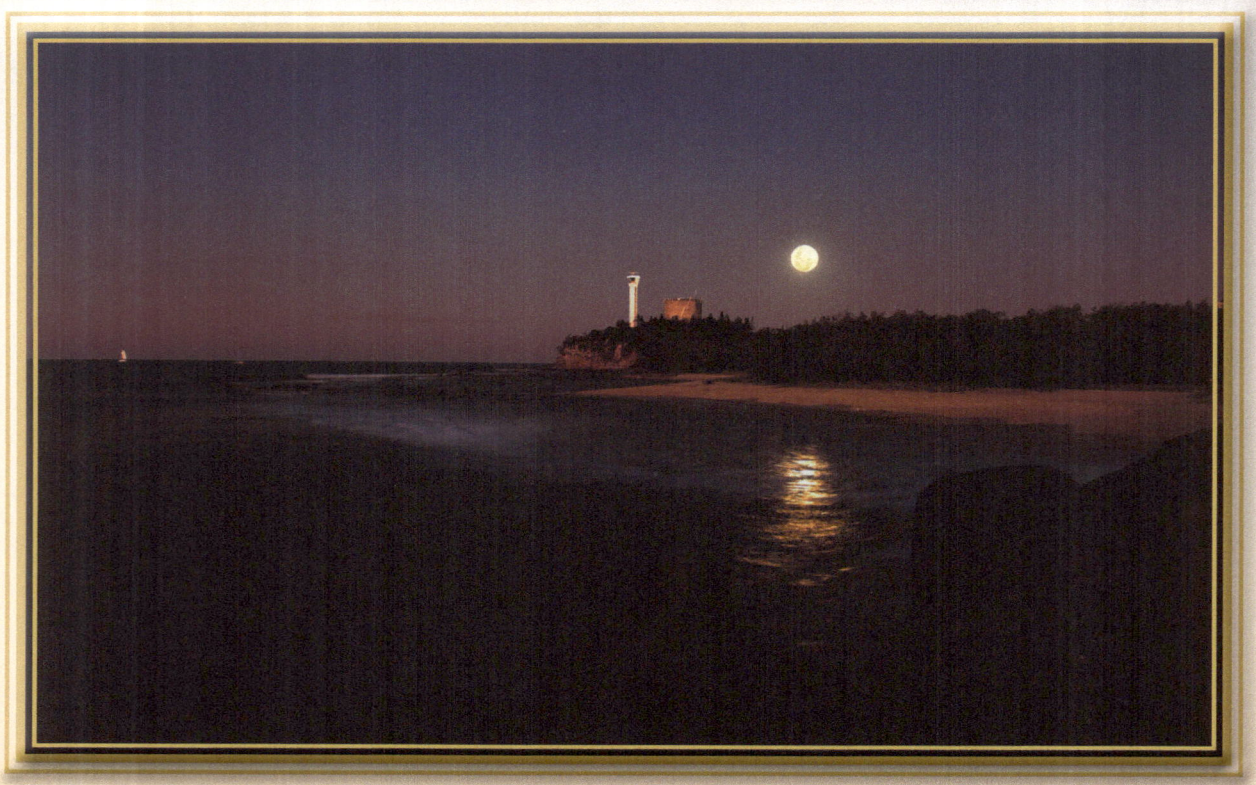

# MOOLOOLABA

Mooloolaba is a suburb and tourist resort township on the Sunshine Coast of Queensland, Australia. It is located 97 kilometres north of the state capital, Brisbane, and is part of the Maroochydore urban centre.

The word "Mooloolaba " derives from the Aboriginal word "mulu", meaning snapper fish, or "mulla" meaning red-bellied black snake. Originally known as Mooloolah Heads, the name was changed to Mooloolaba by Thomas O'Connor in 1919 when he subdivided the land for sale.

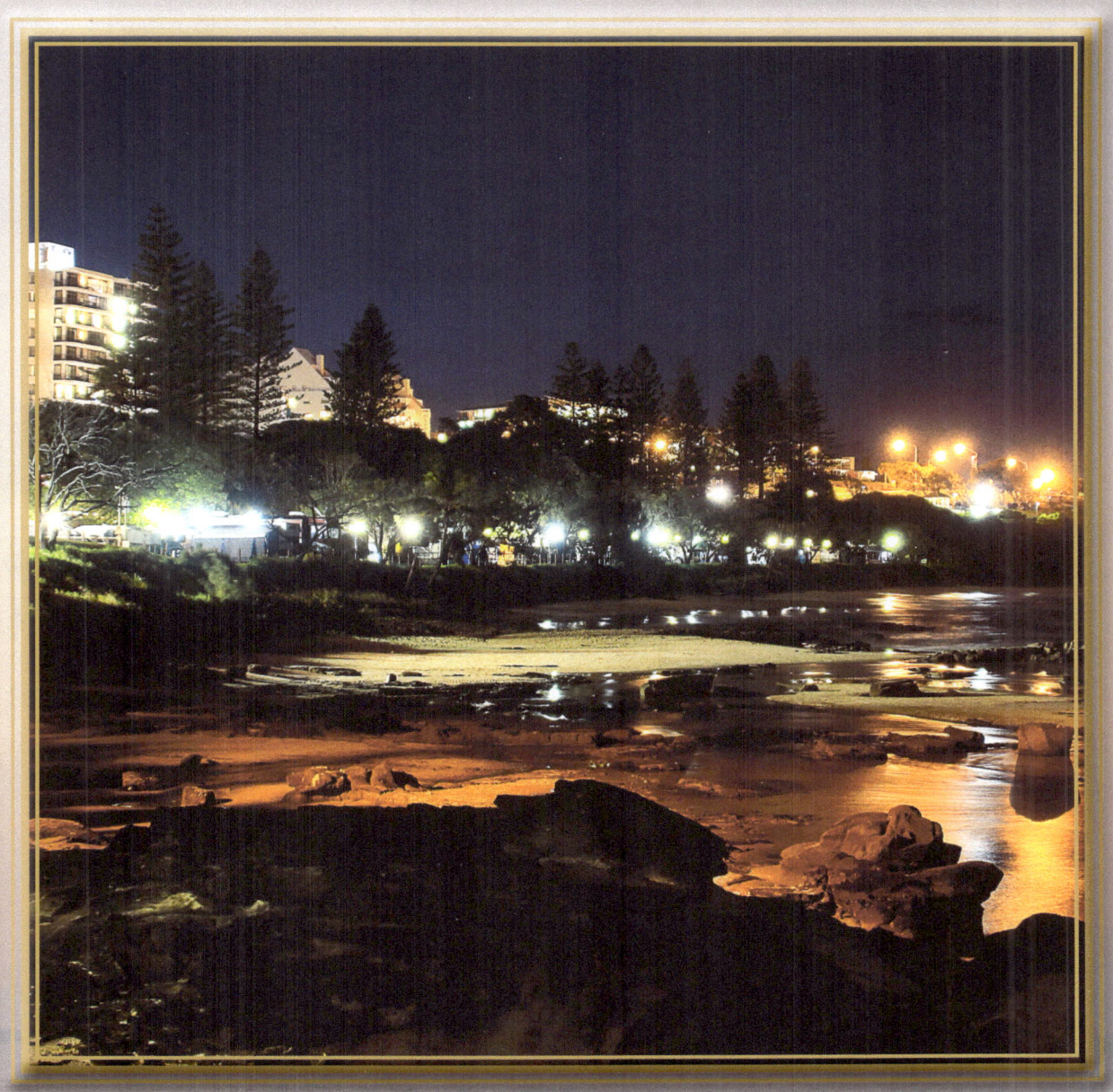

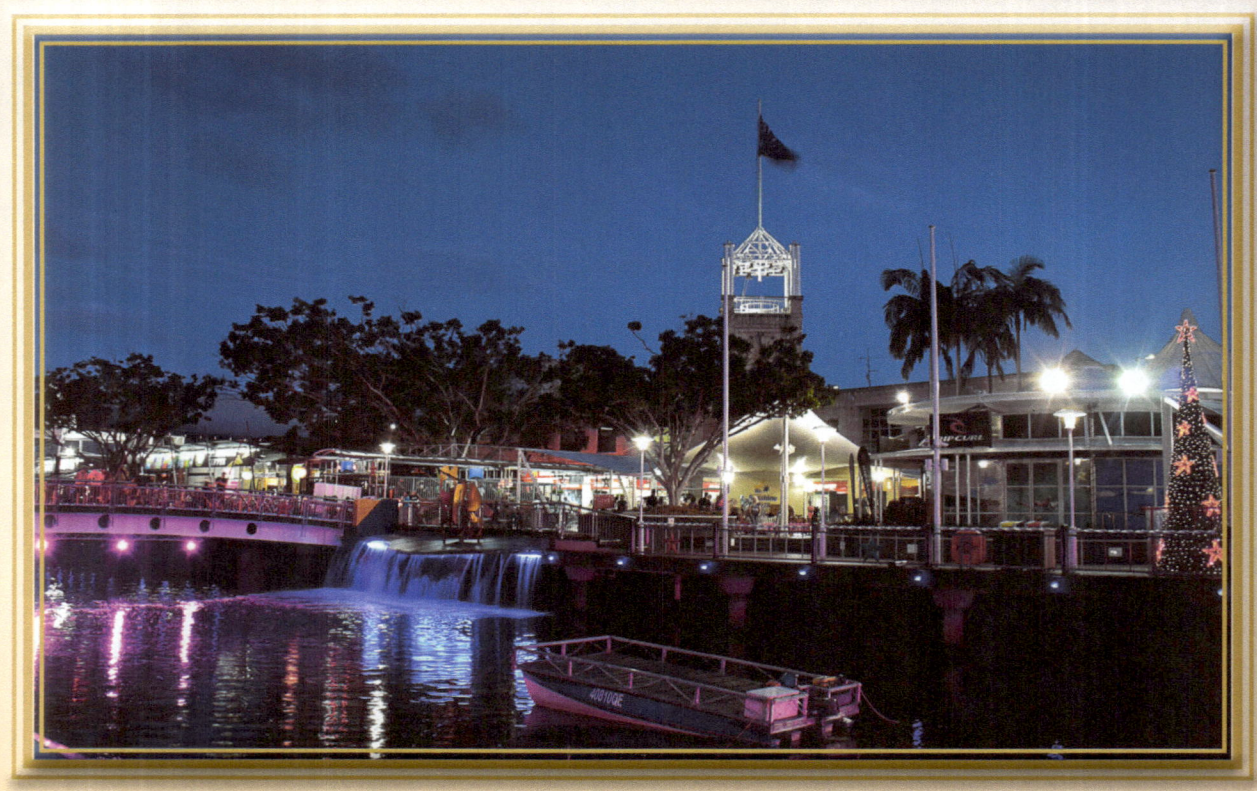

# MAROOCHYDORE

Maroochydore is a major commercial area of the Sunshine Coast with most shopping precincts located in the central business district. It is home to the Sunshine Plaza shopping centre. Maroochydore is also a venue of major surf sport carnivals, and is a popular holiday point from which to travel the rest of Queensland.

The name Maroochydore comes from the Aboriginal indigenous Yuggera language word 'Muru-kutchi', meaning red-bill: the name of the black swan, commonly seen in the area.

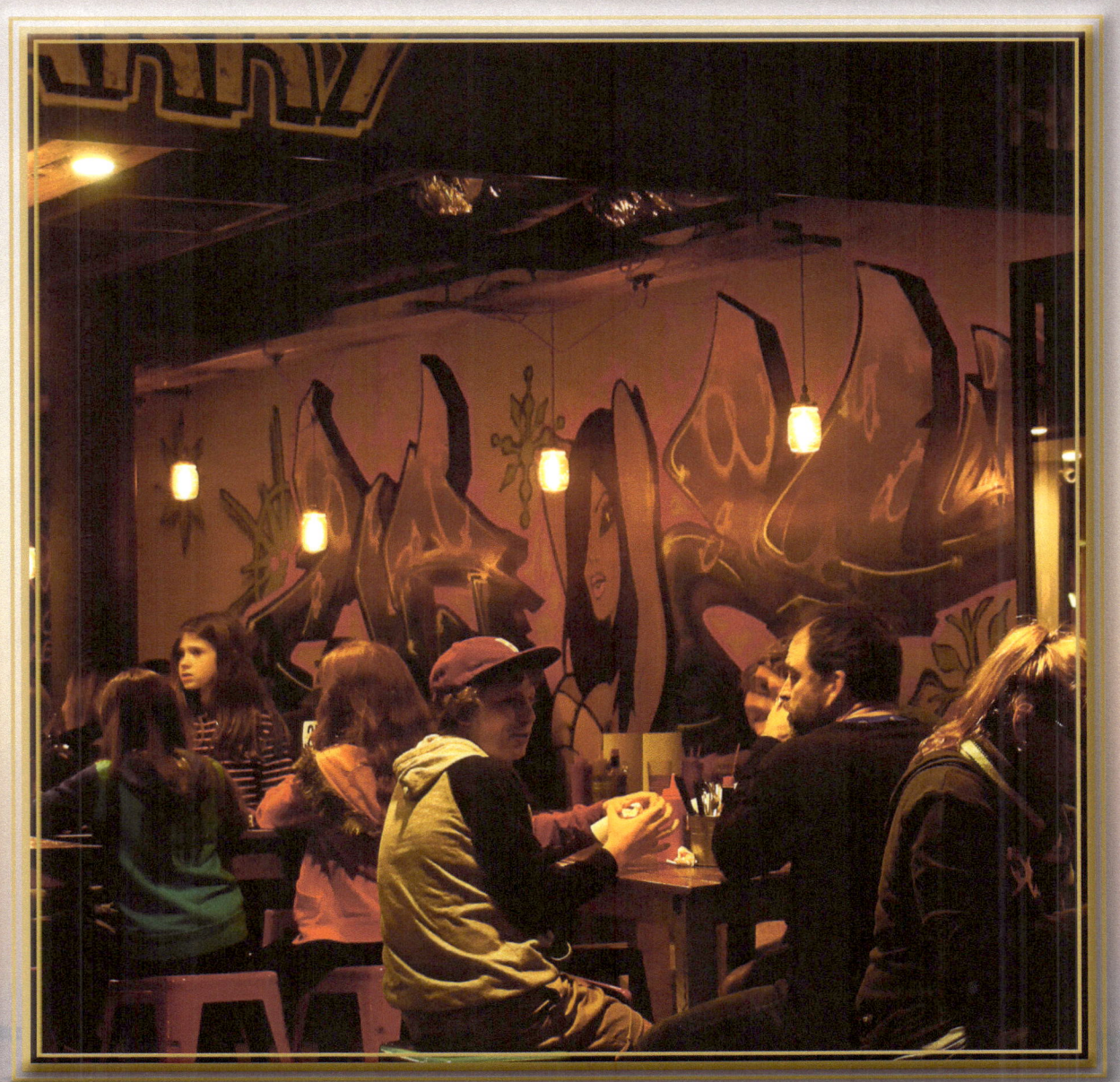

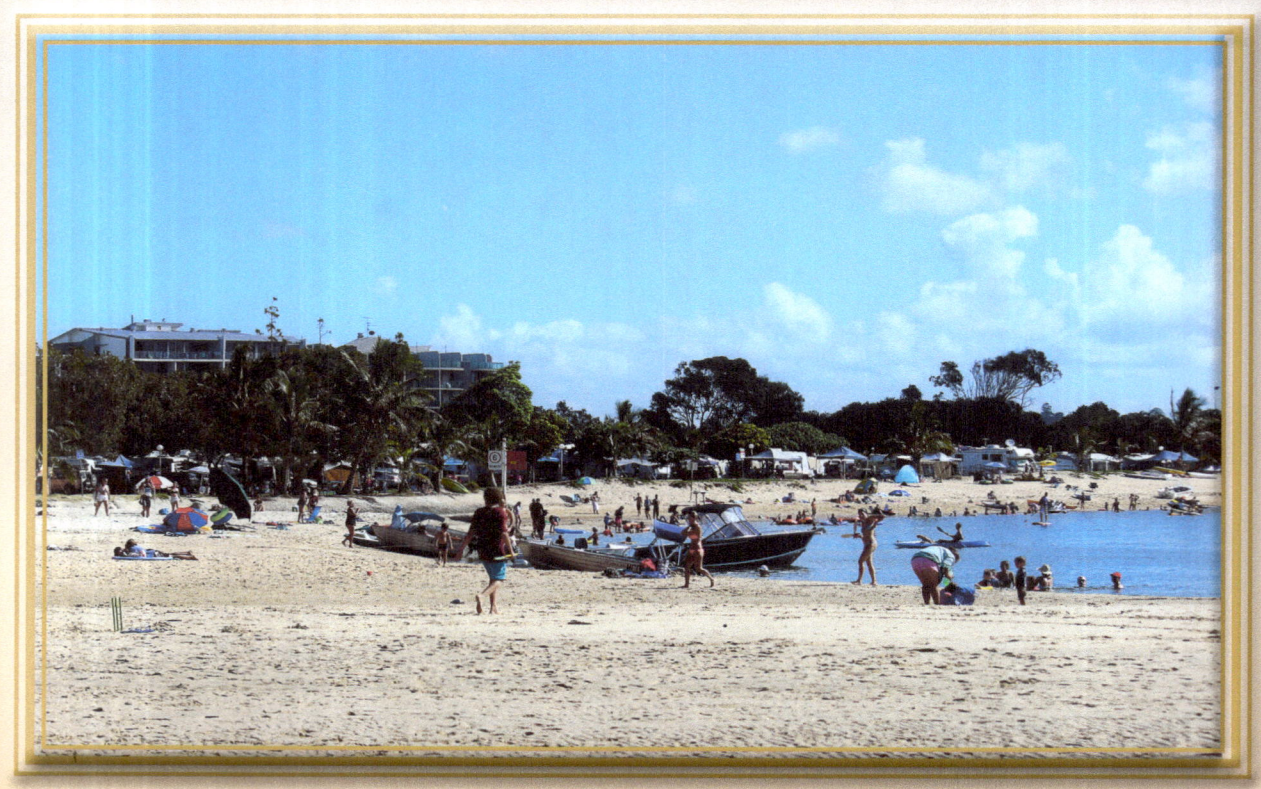

# Cotton Tree

Cotton Tree is a neighbourhood within the suburb of Maroochydore in the Sunshine Coast Region, Queensland, Australia.

Although not officially bounded, Cotton Tree is generally recognised as being bounded by the Maroochy River and Cornmeal Creek to the north, and to the south and west by Aerodrome Road and by the Pacific Ocean to the east.

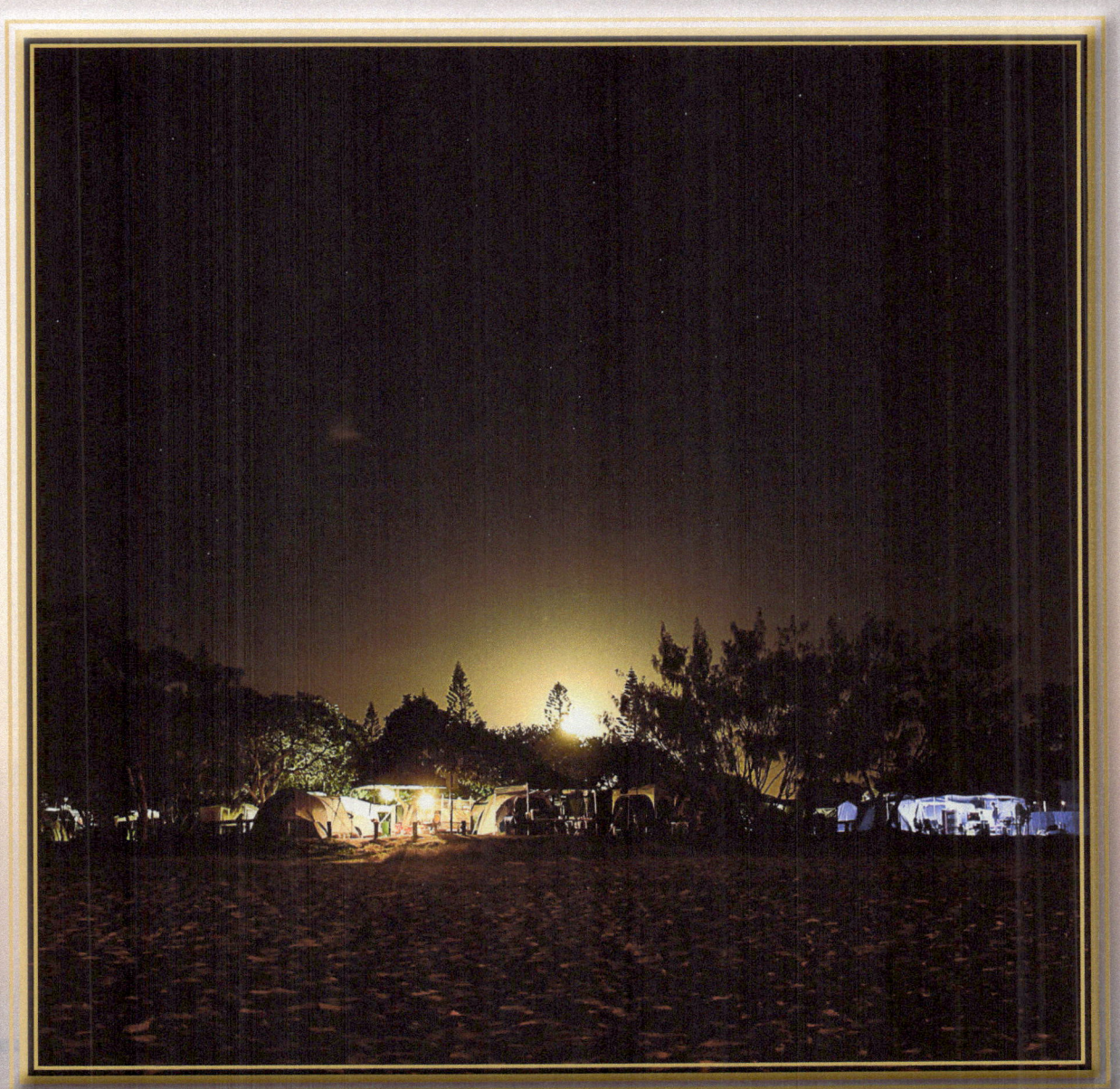

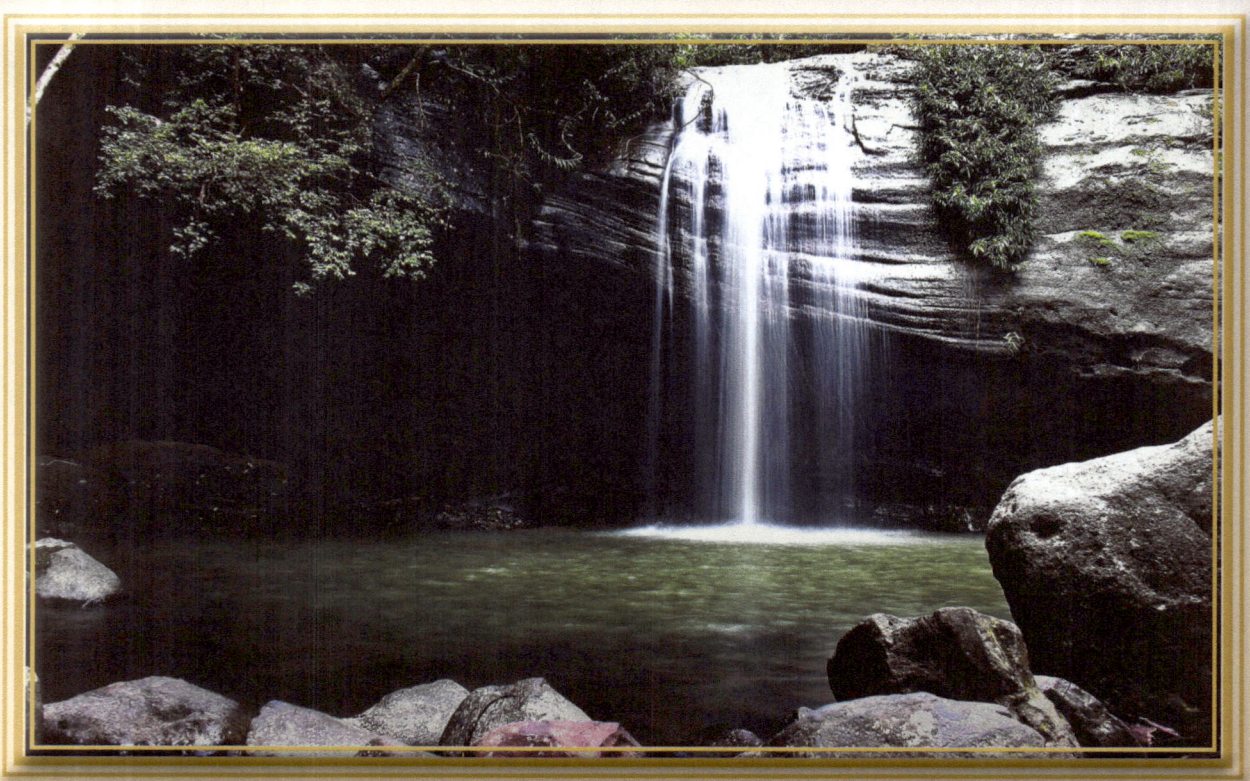

# Buderim

Buderim is an urban centre on the Sunshine Coast, Queensland, Australia. It sits on a 180 metre mountain which overlooks the southern Sunshine Coast communities.

The name "Buderim" is from the local Kabi Kabi Aboriginal word for the hairpin honeysuckle (badderam), Banksia spinulosa var. collina, which grew abundantly in the sandy country around the plateau.

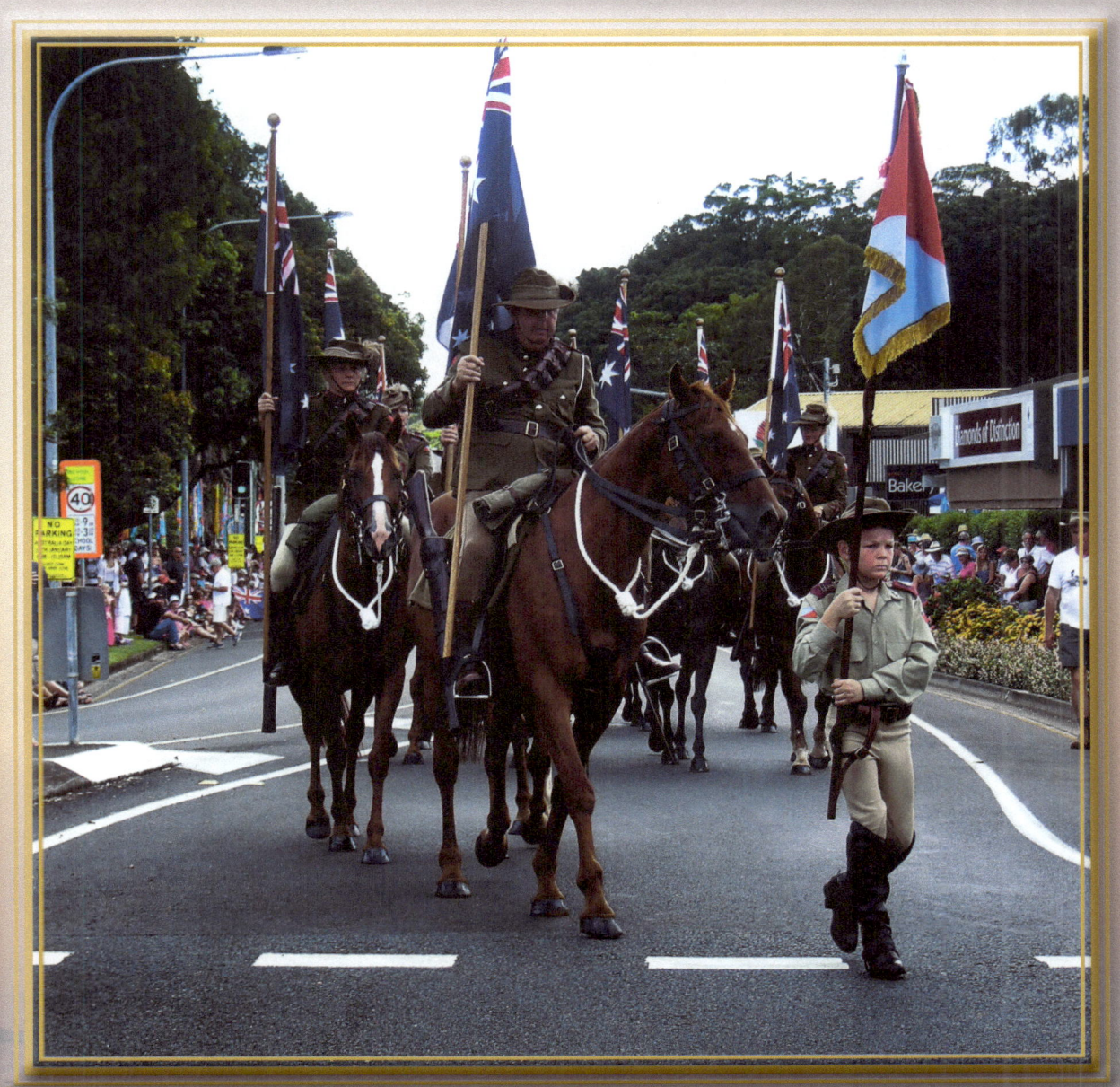

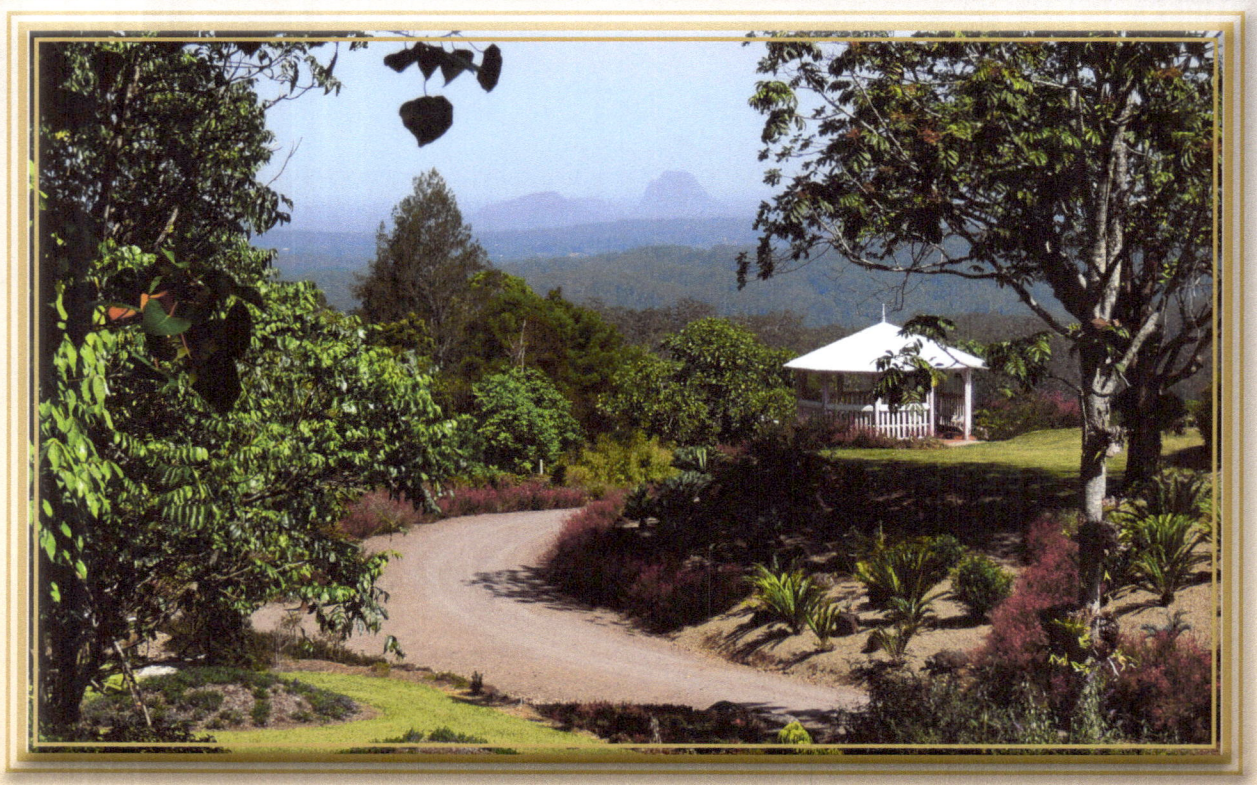

# Maleny

Maleny is a small, scenic town 90 kilometres north of Brisbane on the Blackall Range; situated approximately 450 metres above sea level, amongst the characteristic rolling green hills of the Sunshine Coast Hinterland.

Prior to European settlement, the area was covered in thick sub-tropical rainforest with huge hardwood trees. Timber-getters in the late 19th and early 20th Centuries opened up the area seeking valuable timber, which was priced locally and in Europe.

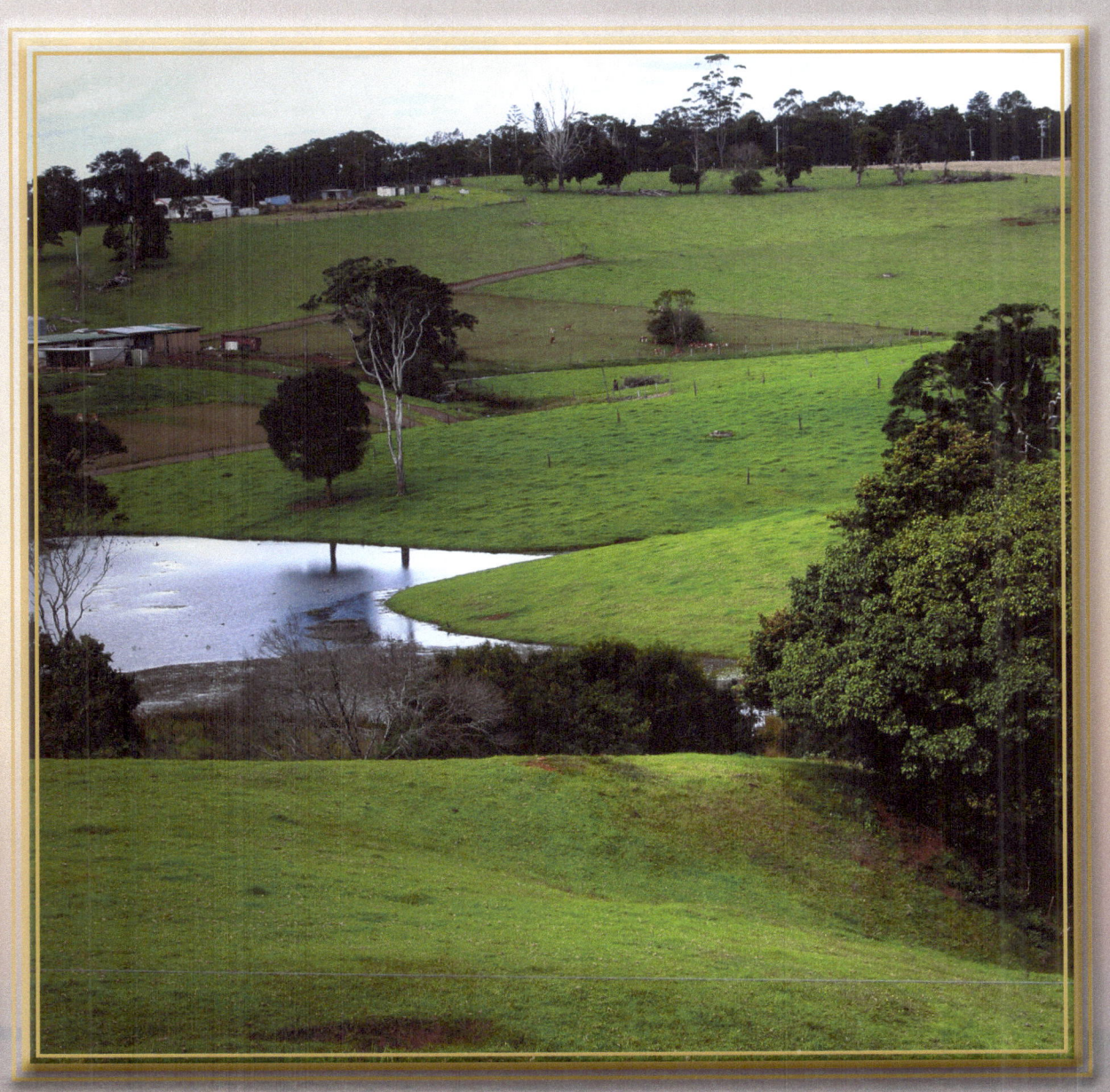

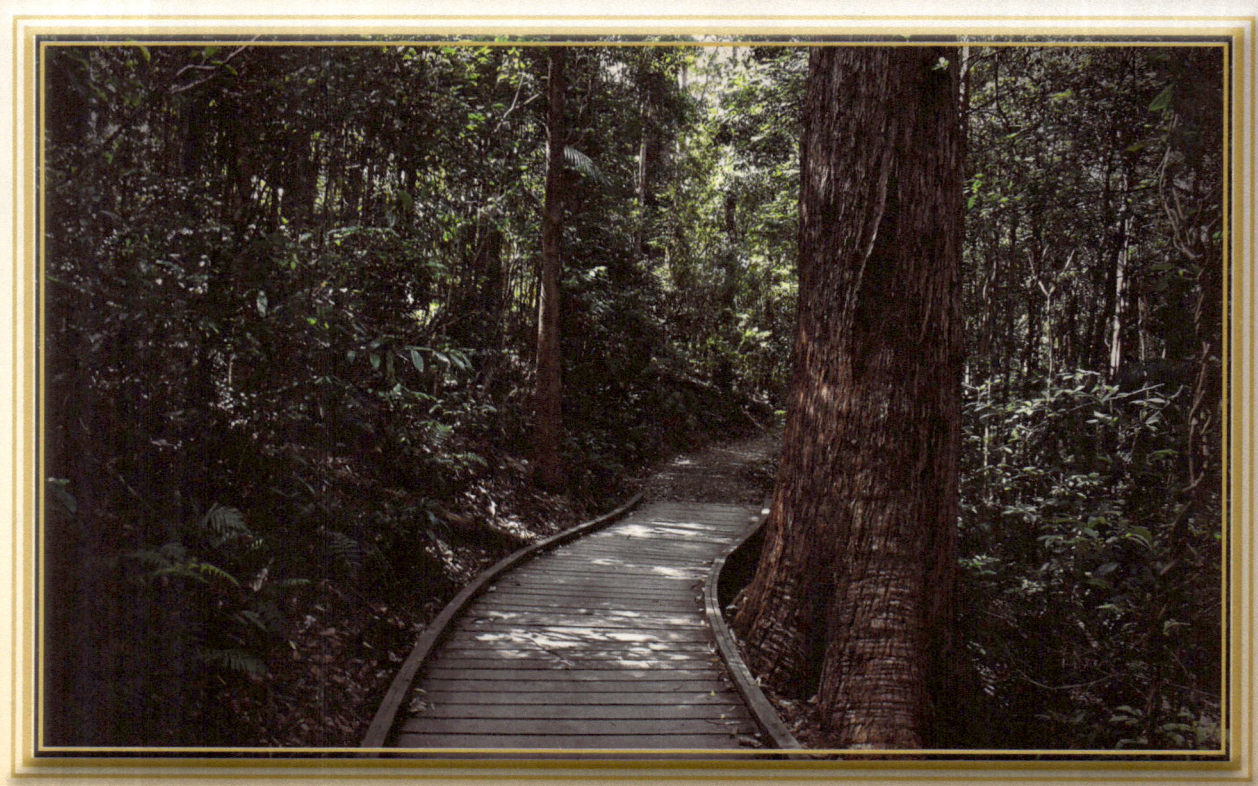

# Kondalilla Falls

Kondalilla is a national park in the Blackall Range of South East Queensland, Australia, 91 kilometres north of Brisbane. William Skene founded this area on his property while searching for lost cattle. He named it Bon Accord before giving it to the Queensland Government who, during the 50's, renamed it Kondalilla which is an Aboriginal word for running water. The area was first officially protected in 1906 as a recreational area, becoming a national park in 1945.

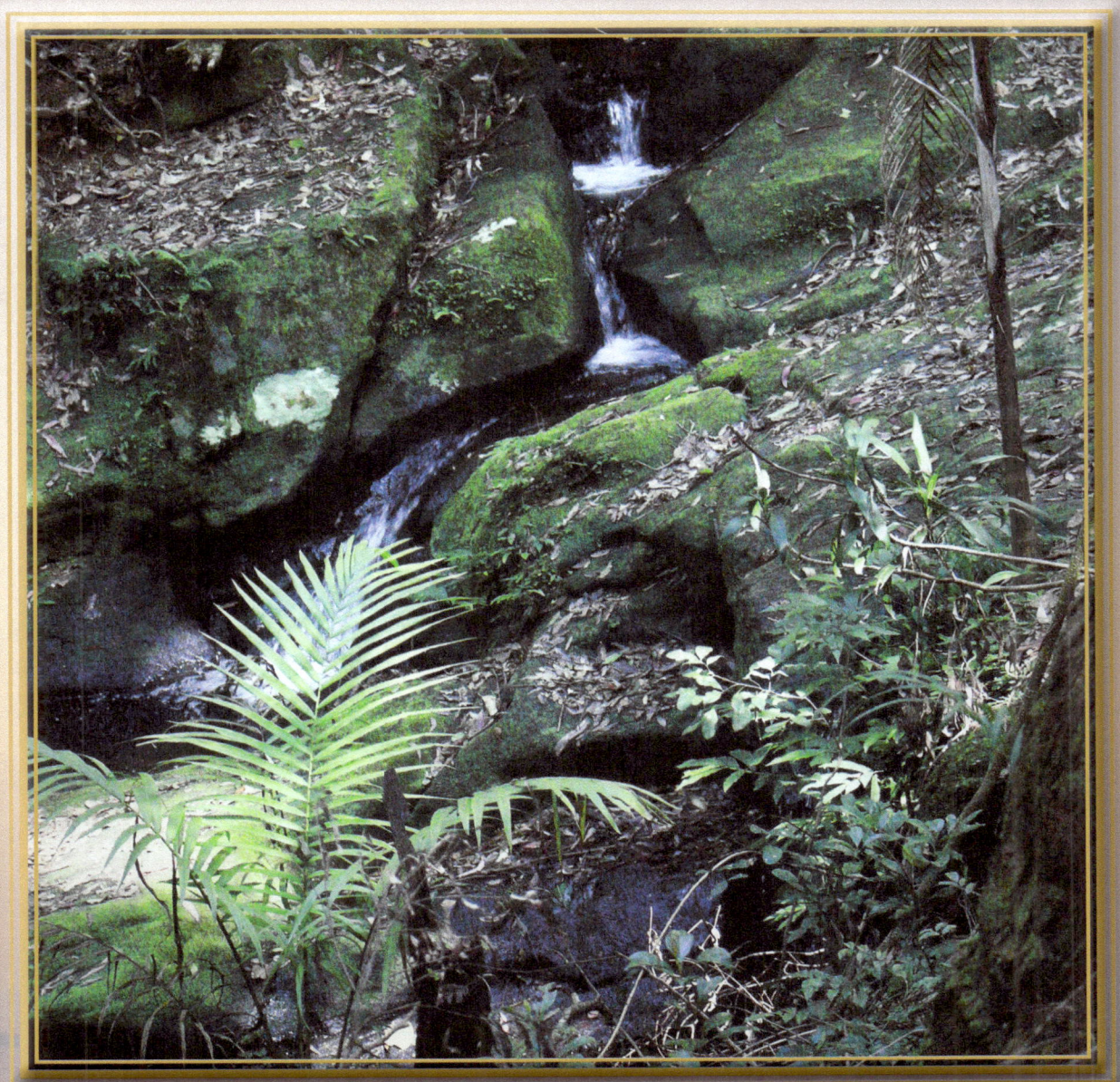

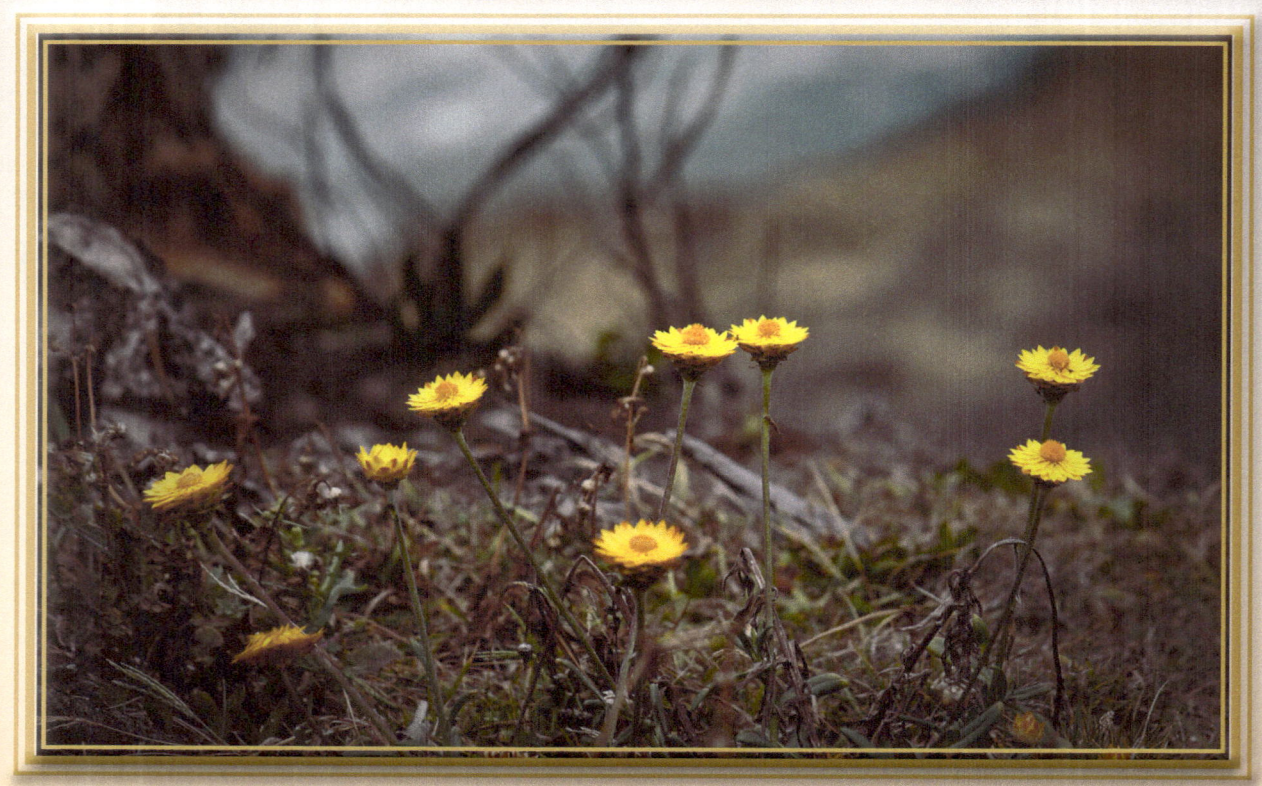

# Noosa National Park

Noosa National Park is a national park in Queensland, Australia, 121 kilometres north of Brisbane. It is situated near Noosa Heads between the Pacific Ocean and the Sunshine Coast's northern area of urban development and extends southwards, past Lake Weyba to Coolum.

Several beaches in the park provide good locations for swimming. These beaches are not patrolled. Swimmers should be aware of strong currents at Alexandria Bay. The southern end of Alexandria Bay is unofficially clothing optional.

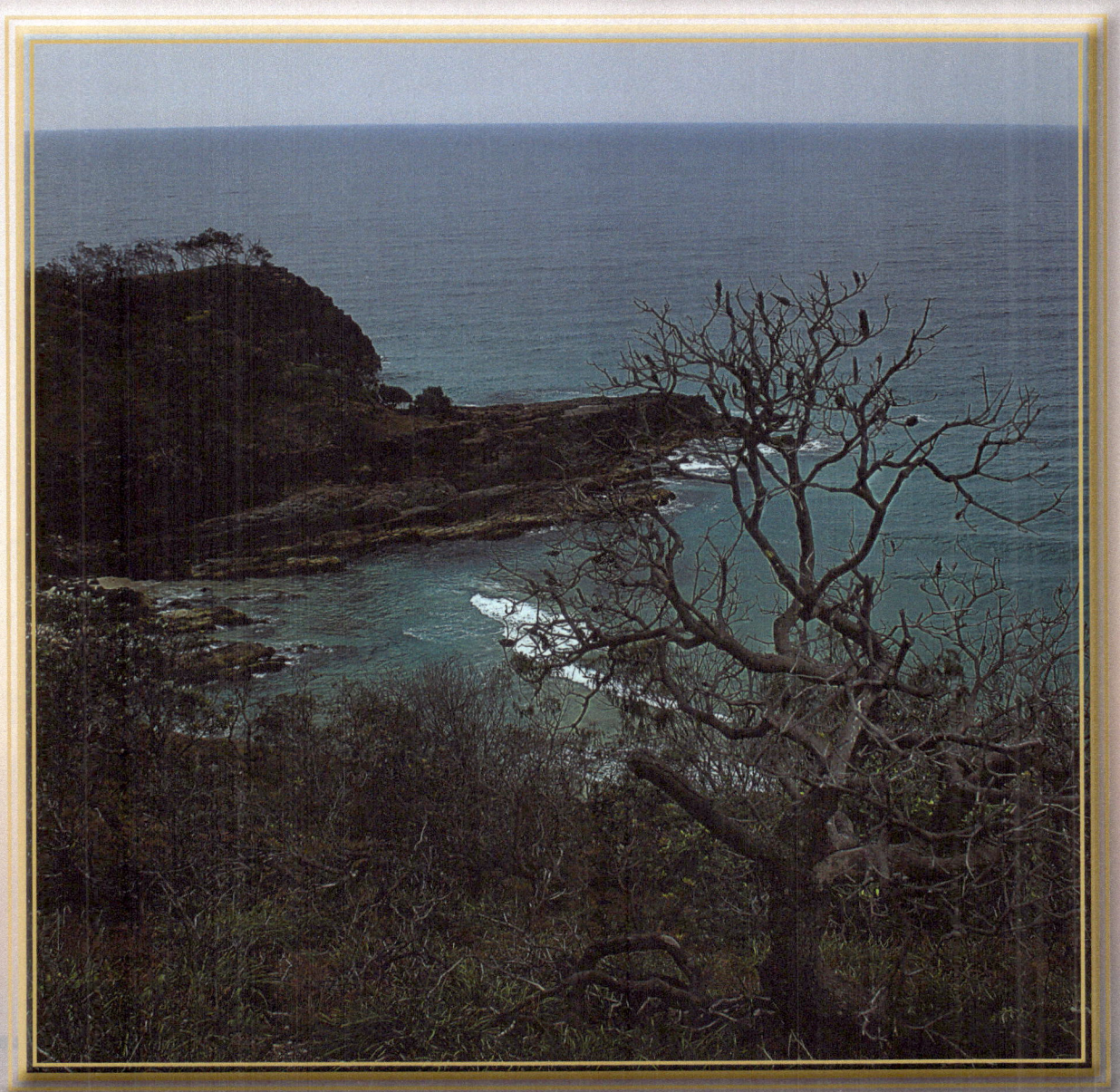

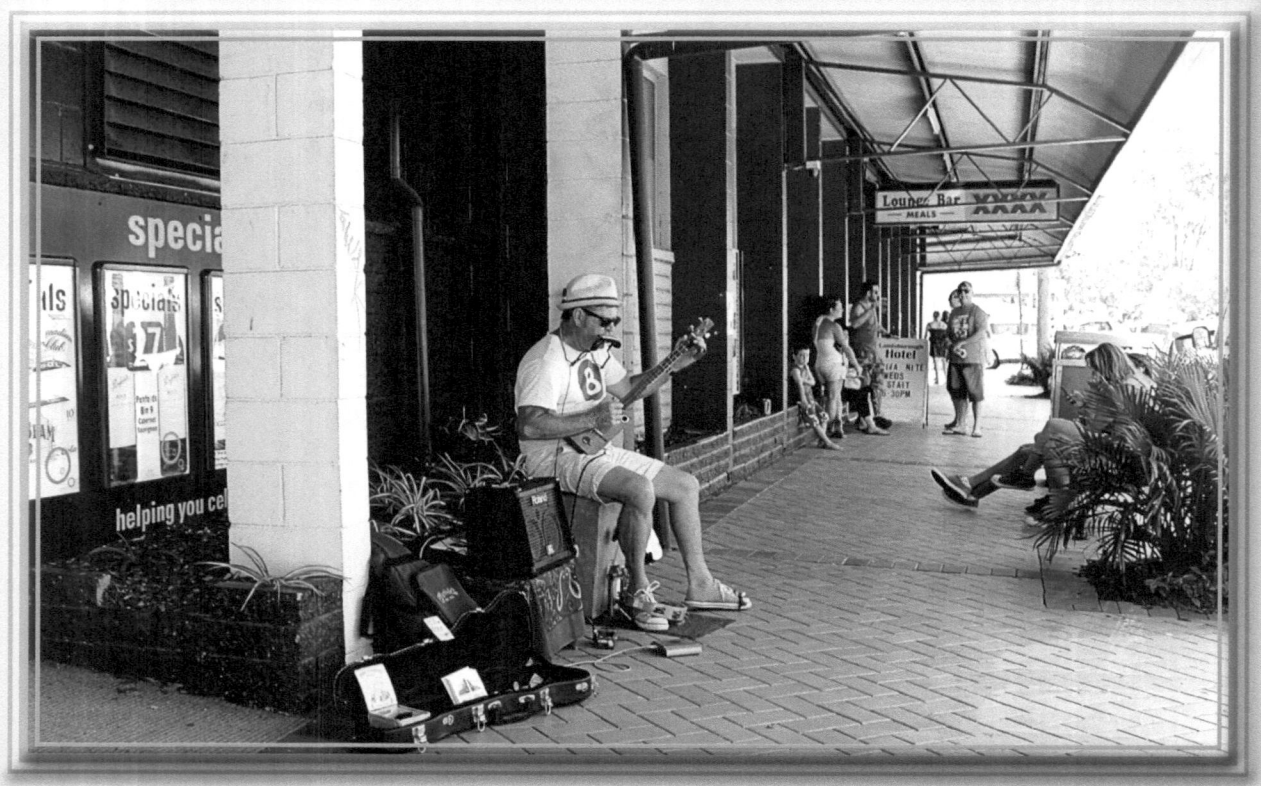

# Landsborough

Landsborough is a small town on the Sunshine Coast Hinterland of Queensland, Australia. It is situated north of the Glasshouse Mountains just off Steve Irwin Way, 82 kilometres north of Brisbane at the base of the southern end of the Blackall Range.

Landsborough is situated on the North Coast railway line from Brisbane and there are several services daily southbound to Brisbane and northbound to Nambour and Gympie.

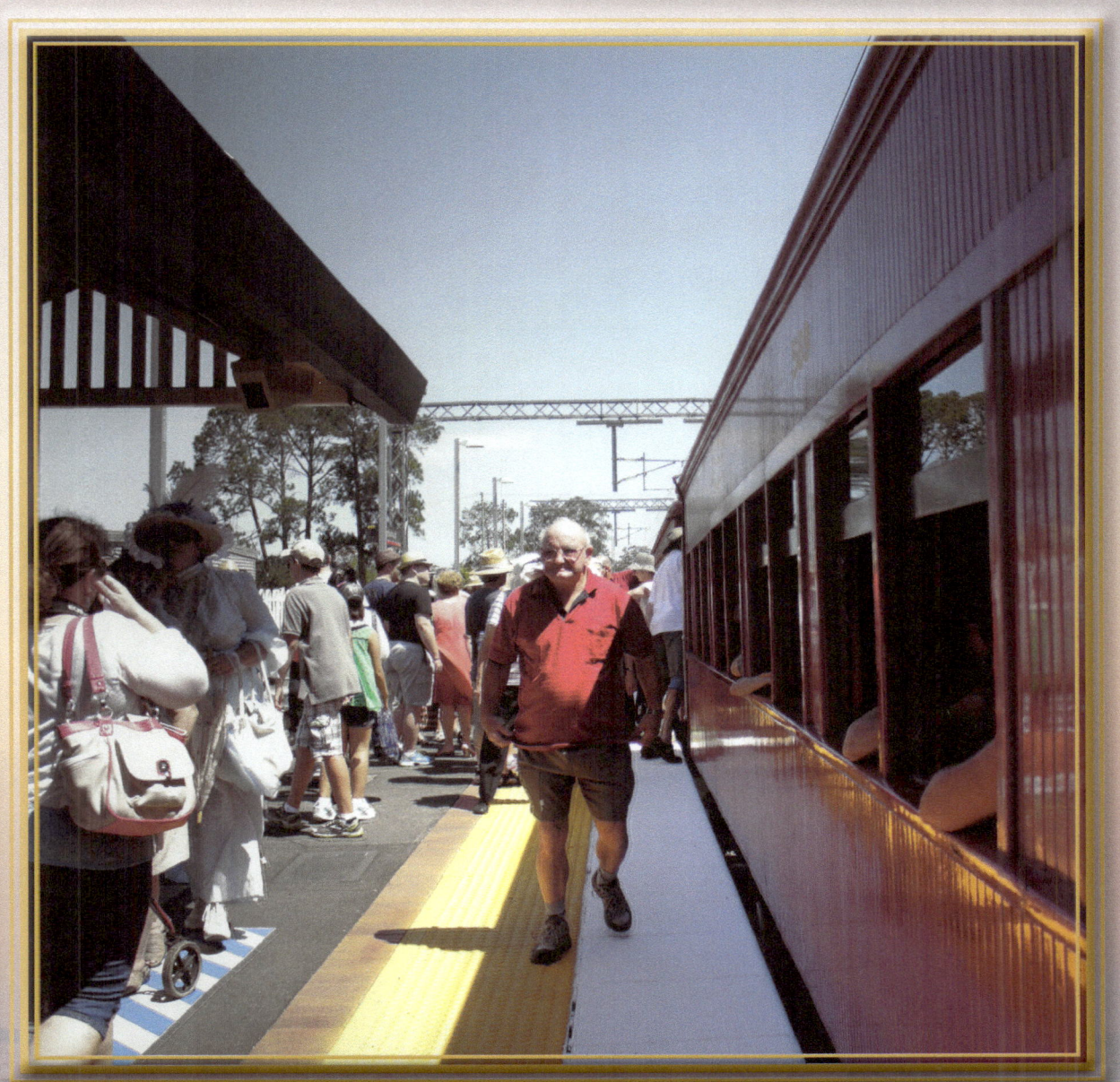

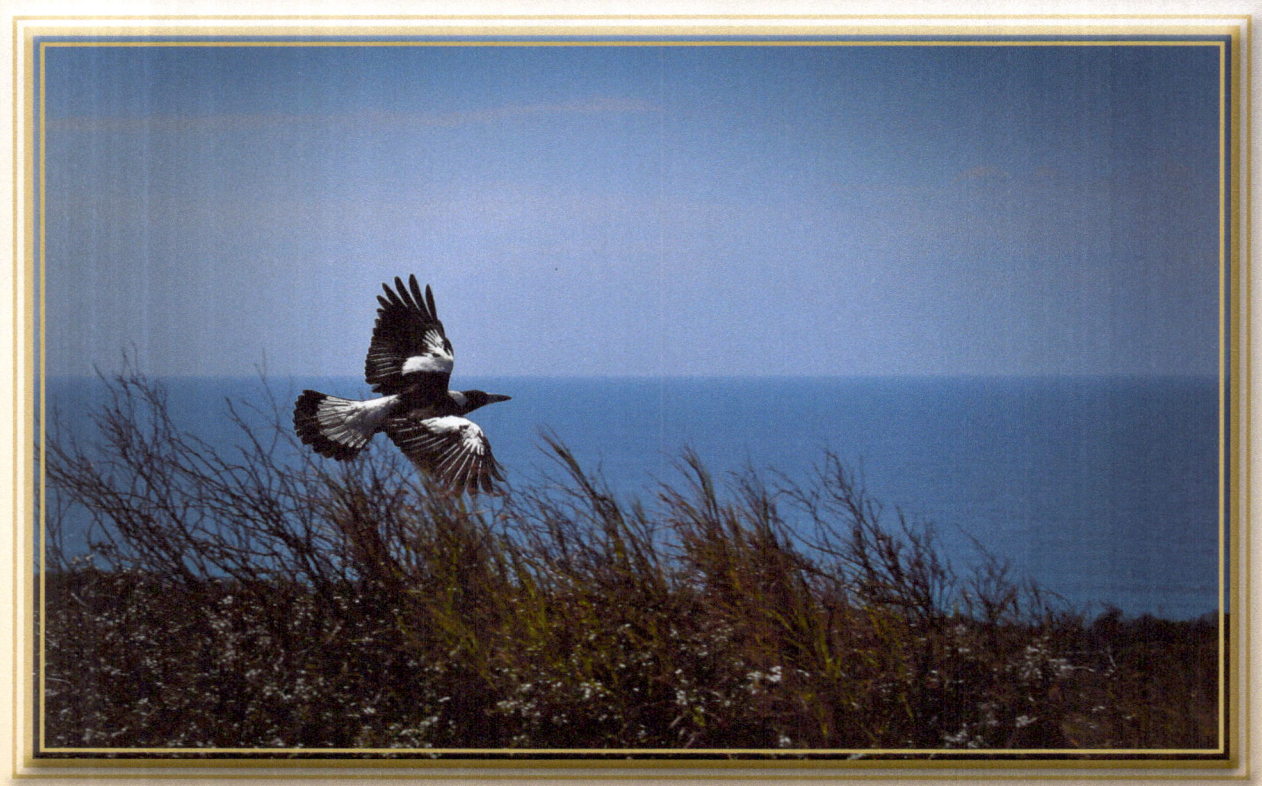

# Mount Emu

Situated between Coolum and Peregian Beach, Mount Emu gets its name from the local Aboriginal word "peregian" which means emu. This is an easy walk up a fairly rutted path and a leisurely pace will see you at the top in about 20 minutes.

During the best whale watching month, October, Mount Emu is an excellent spot to see pods of whales beaching just a few hundred metres from the shoreline.

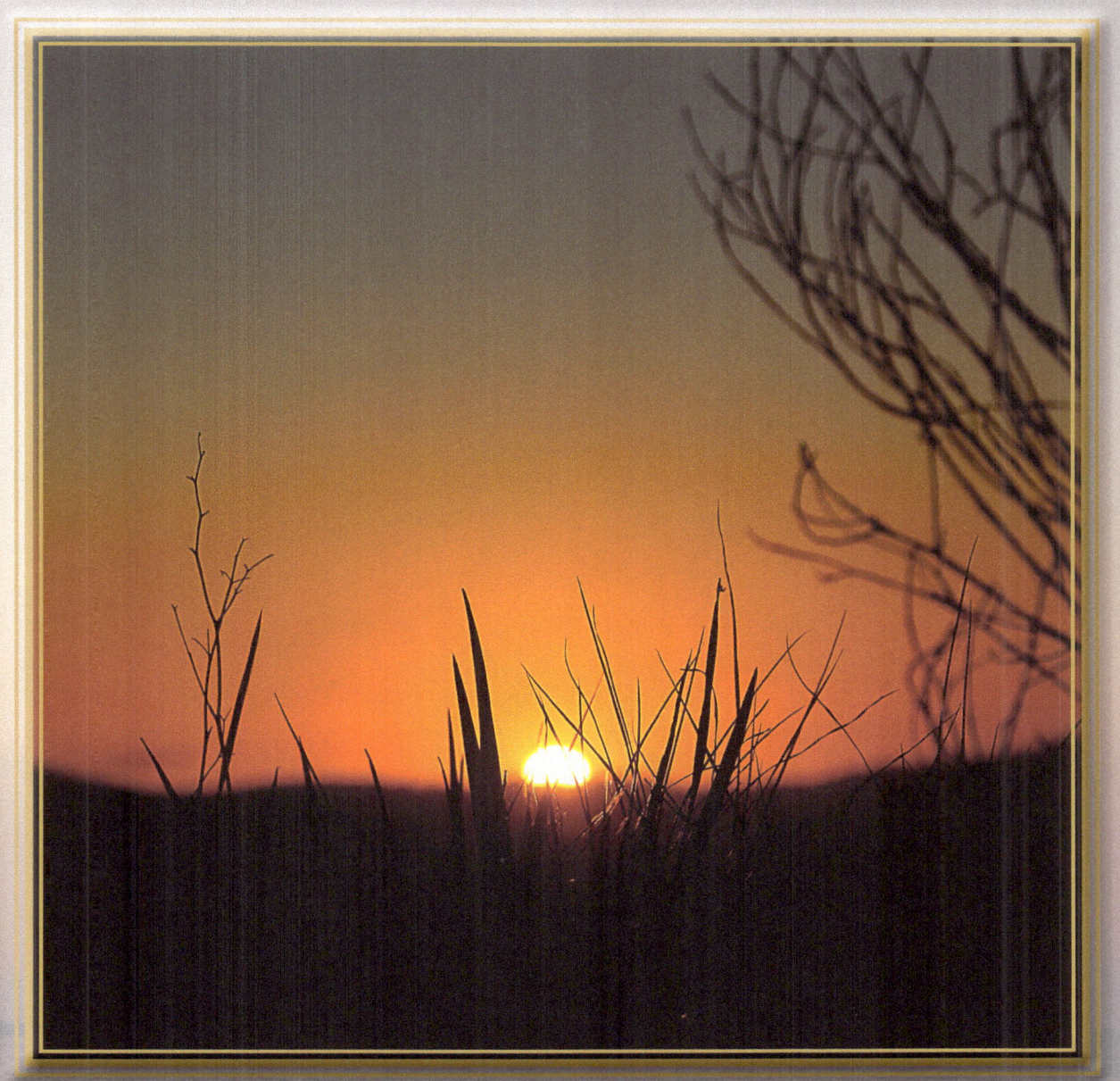

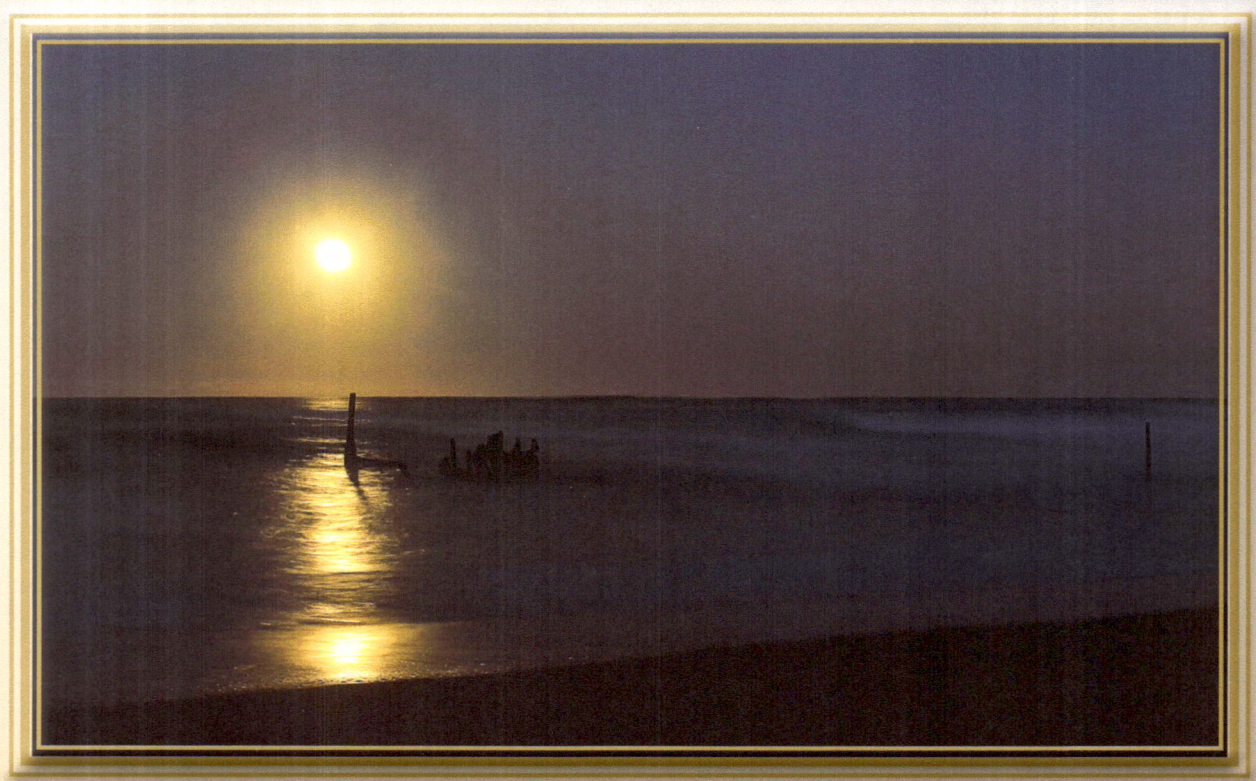

# Dicky Beach

Dicky Beach is both a beach and suburb of the Sunshine Coast Region, Queensland, Australia, located within the Caloundra urban centre.

The area was named after the iron steamboat, the SS Dicky, which ran aground during heavy seas on 12th February 1893. It was re-floated, but heavy seas turned the ship about and back onto the sand where it remained. Dicky Beach remains the only recreational beach in the world to be named after a shipwreck.

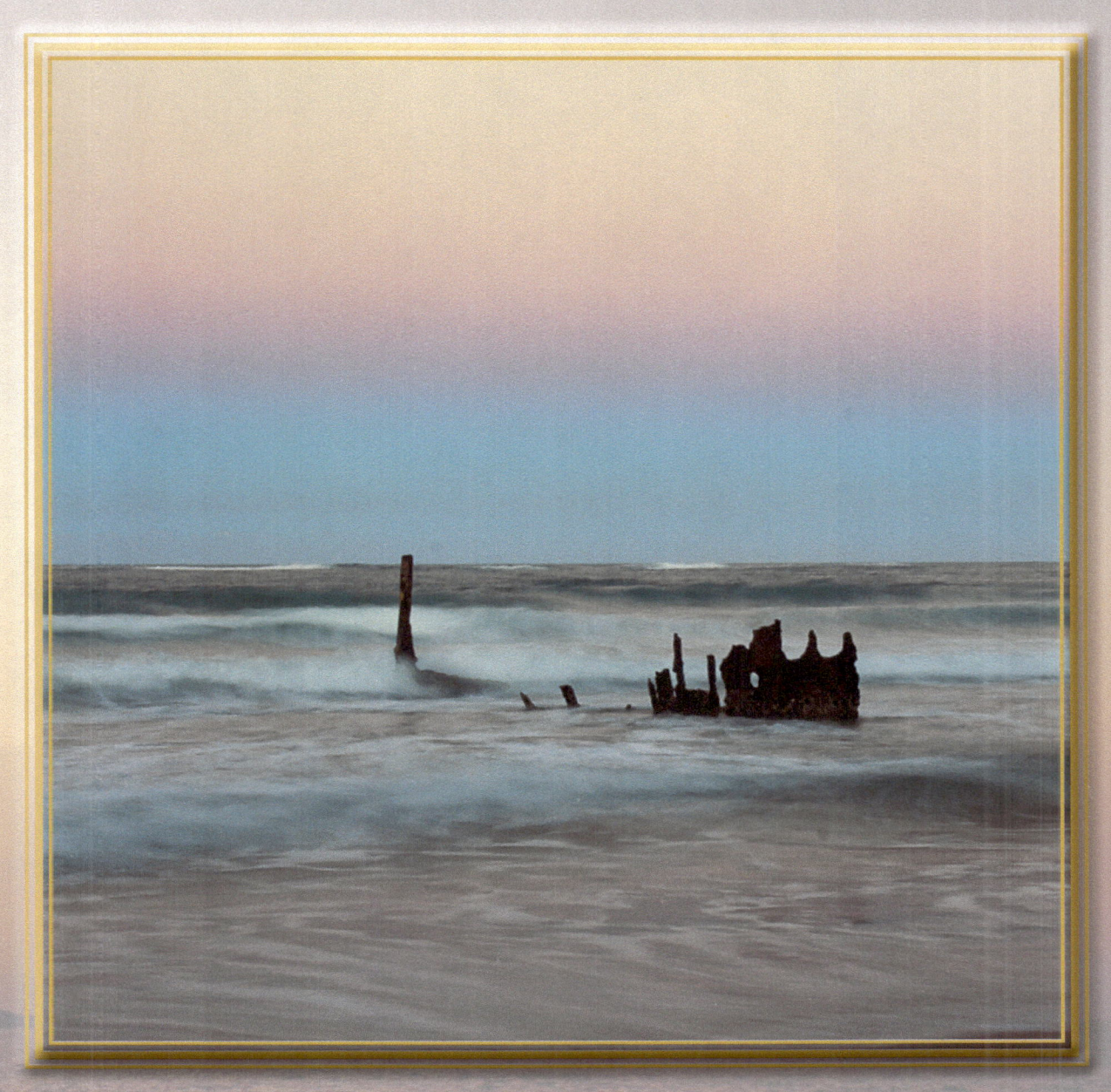

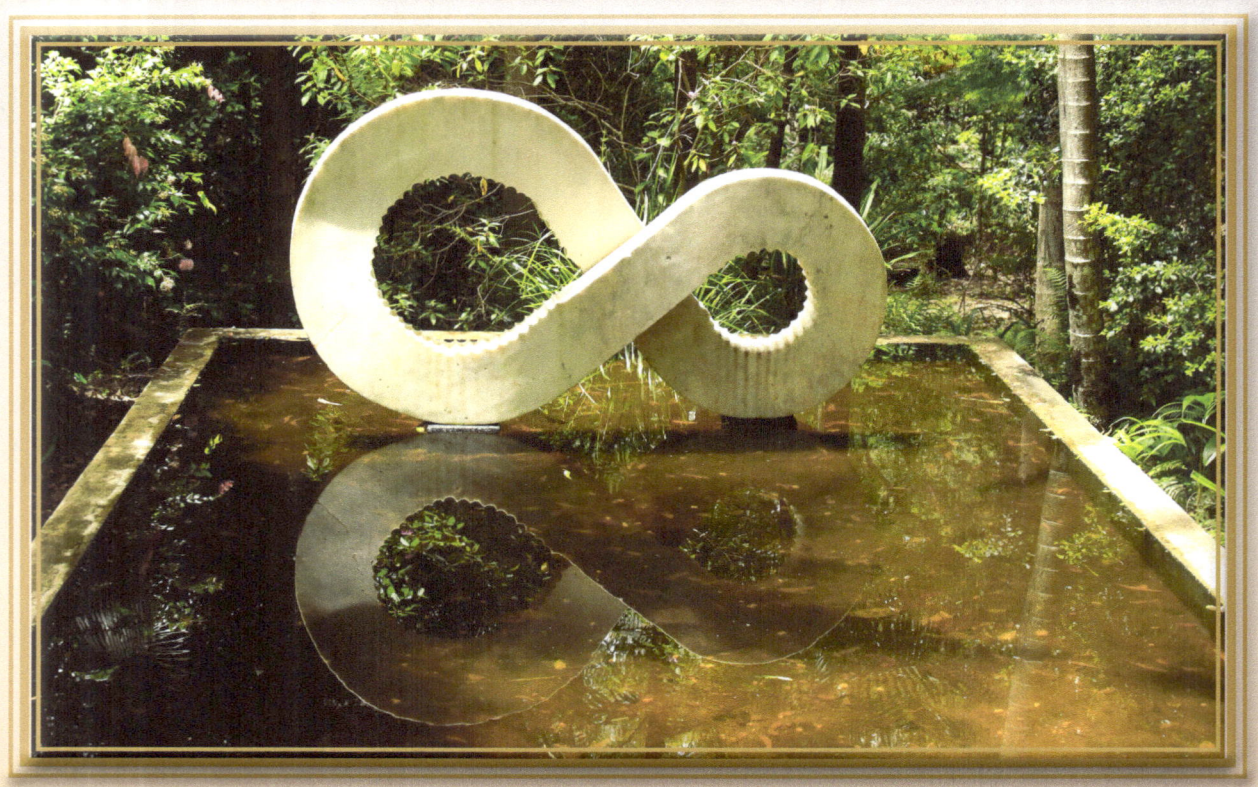

# Maroochy Bushland Botanic Gardens

In the gardens, there are a number of concrete paths and well developed gravel paths which allow access to much of the developed part of the gardens for strollers and wheelchairs, providing an experience of harmony between humans and the living earth.

The Maroochy Regional Bushland Botanic Gardens are located on Palm Creek Road, Tanawha, beside the Tanawha Golf Course.

Sourse: www.sunshinecoast.qld.gov.au

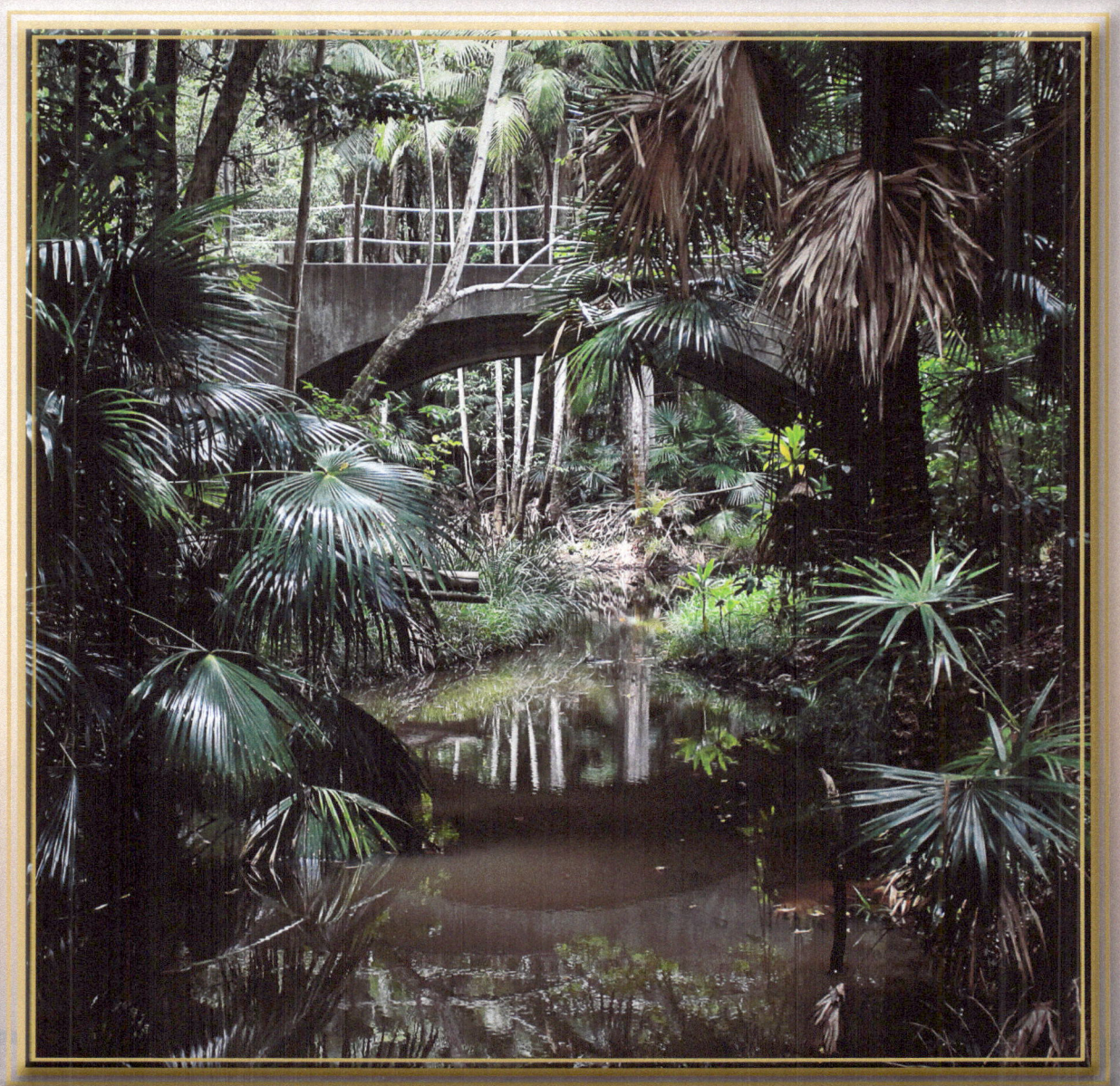

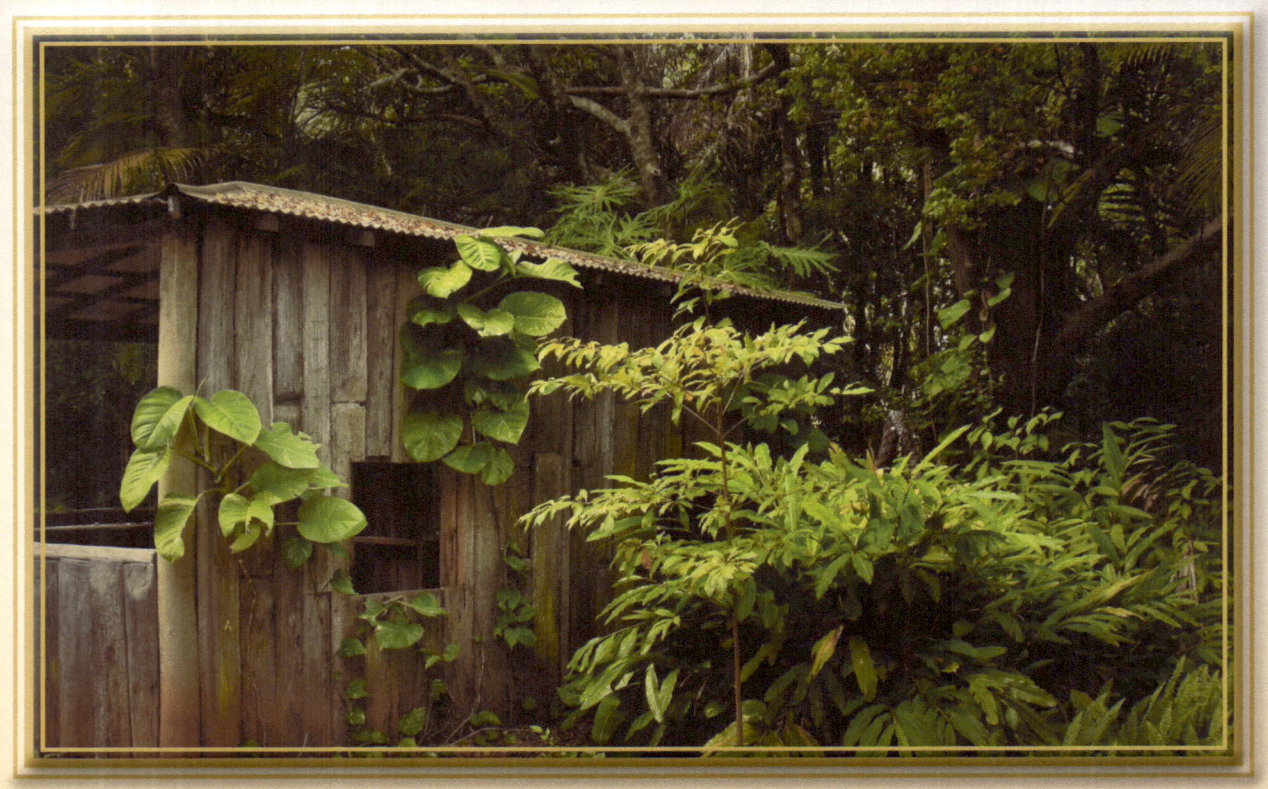

# Buderim Ginger Factory - Yandina

The Buderim Ginger Factory is a tourist attraction & working ginger factory established in 1980. There are rides, tours of the factory, and shops, restaurants and other exhibits for visitors to enjoy.

The Buderim Ginger Factory is operated by Buderim Ginger Ltd that was listed as a public company in December 1988. The company manufactures confectionery ginger products that are marketed in Australia and exported to a number of countries including UK, USA, Canada & some European countries.

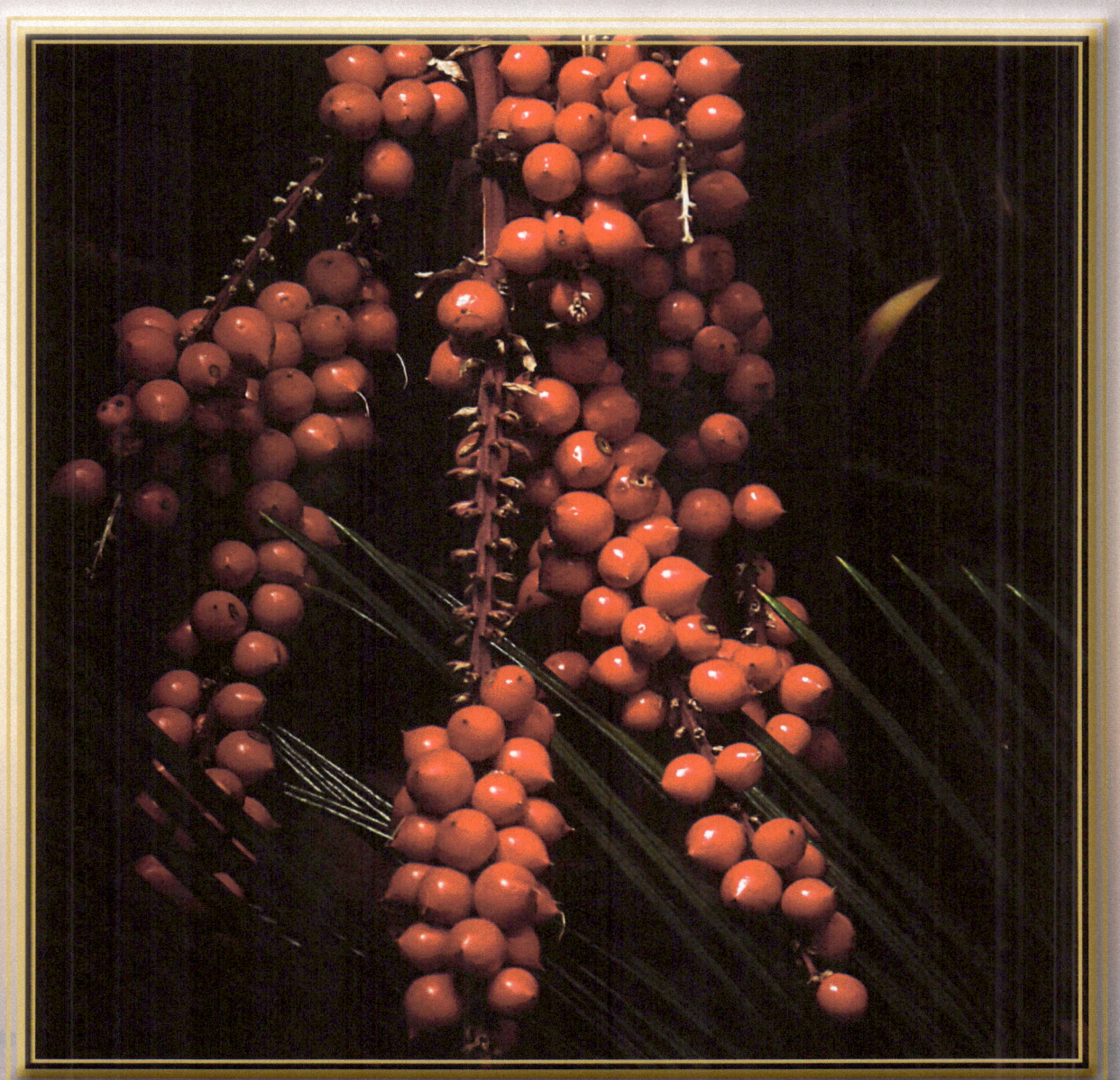

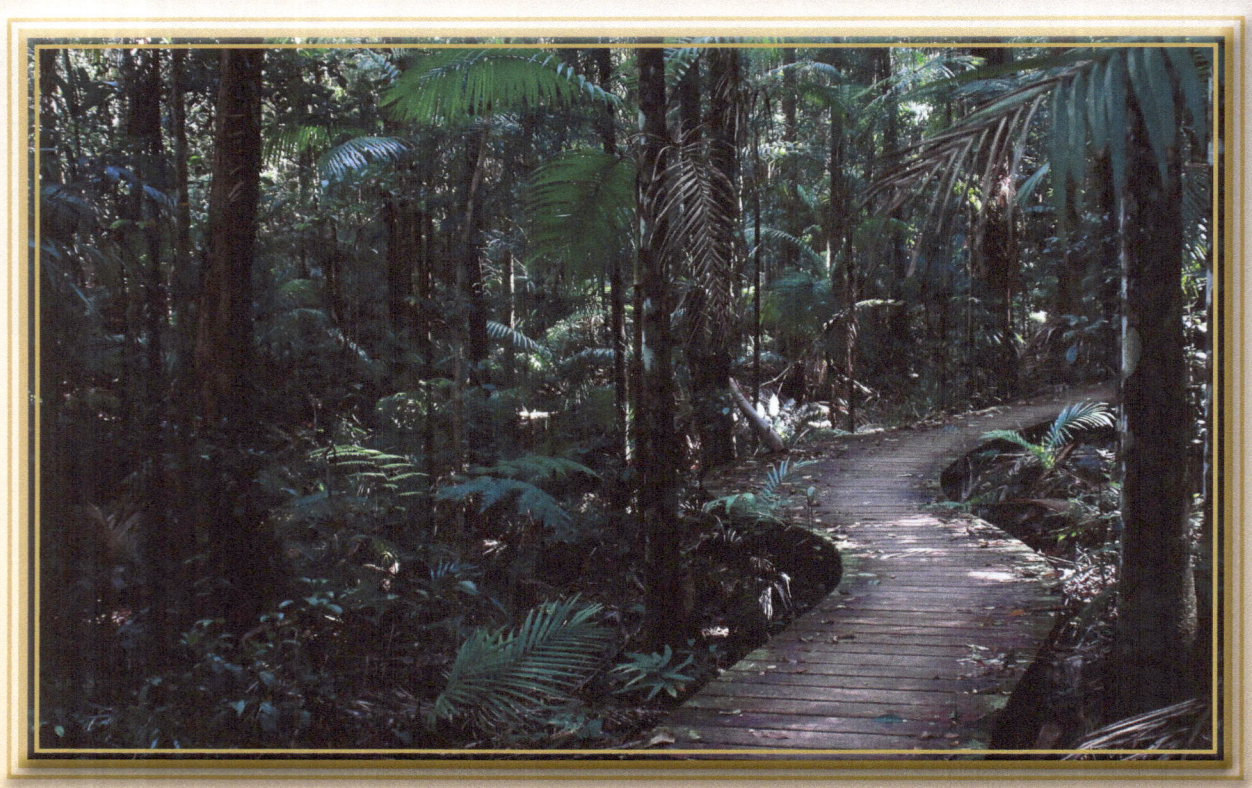

# Baroon Pocket Dam - Montville

The Baroon Pocket Dam is a rock and earth-filled embankment dam with an ungated spillway across the Obi Obi Creek, which is located in the South East region of Queensland, Australia. The main purpose of the dam is for portable water supply. The resultant reservoir is called Lake Baroon.

Just below the dam is Obi Obi Gorge, one of the few remaining places left where the Mary River cod maintains a wild population.

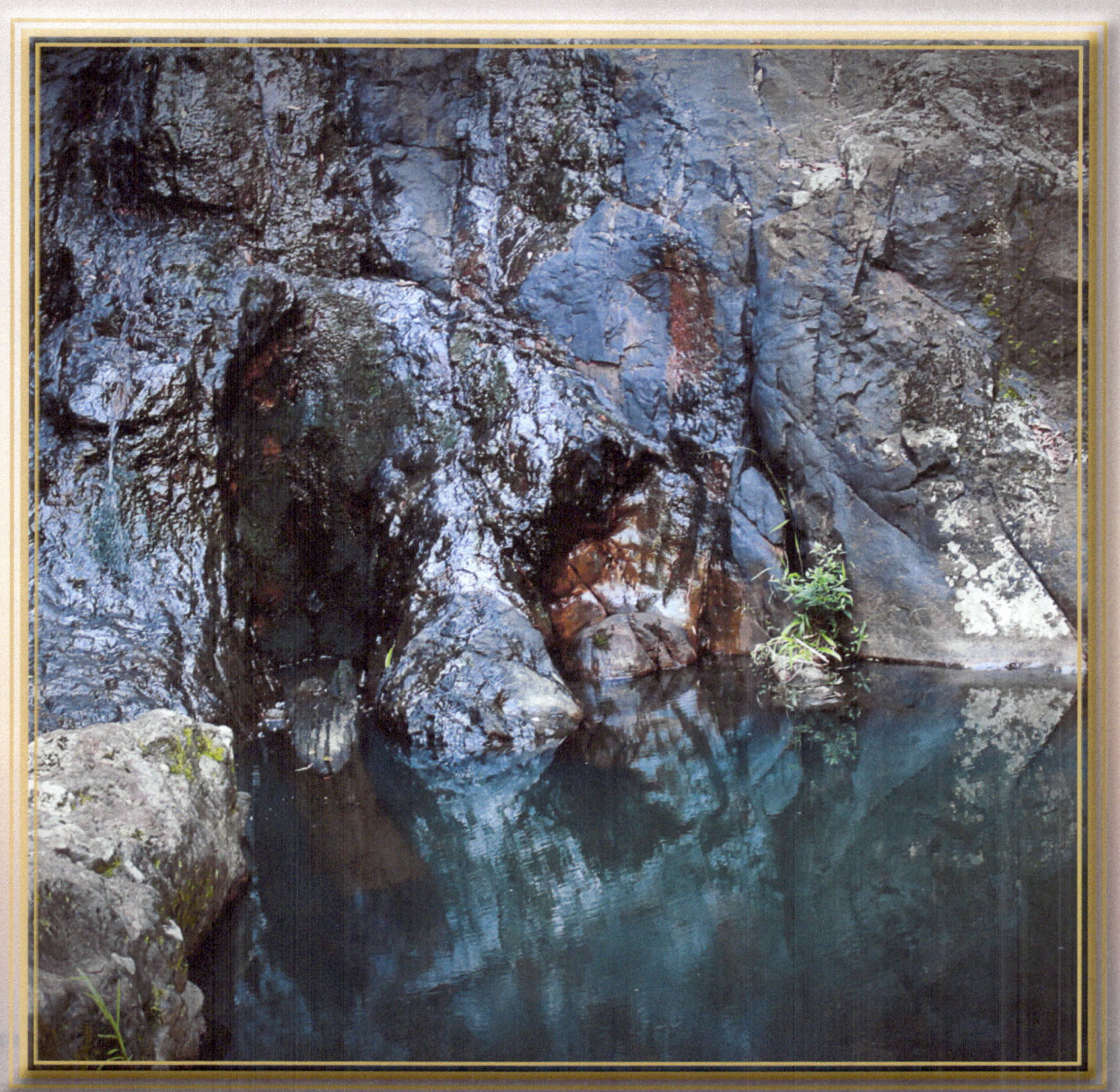

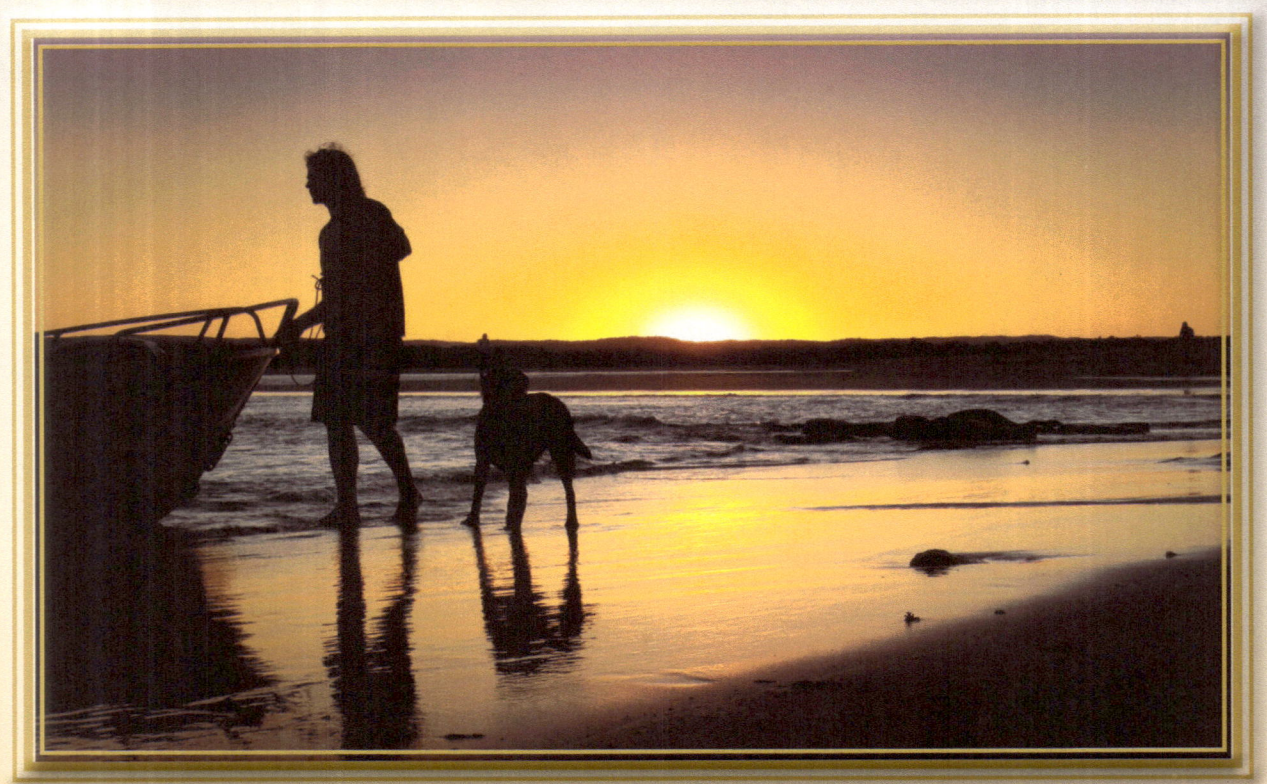

# Pincushion Island

Pincushion Island is pretty small and is only accessible from the beach at low tide. It is surrounded by water at high tide though, so it still counts as an island!

At low tide, Pincushion Island becomes a fun spot to climb around the rocks, marvel at the powerful waves, and take in the great views. Climb to the top of Pincushion Island for a nice vantage point of where the Maroochydore River meets the ocean.

Sourse: www.sweethomeaustralia.com

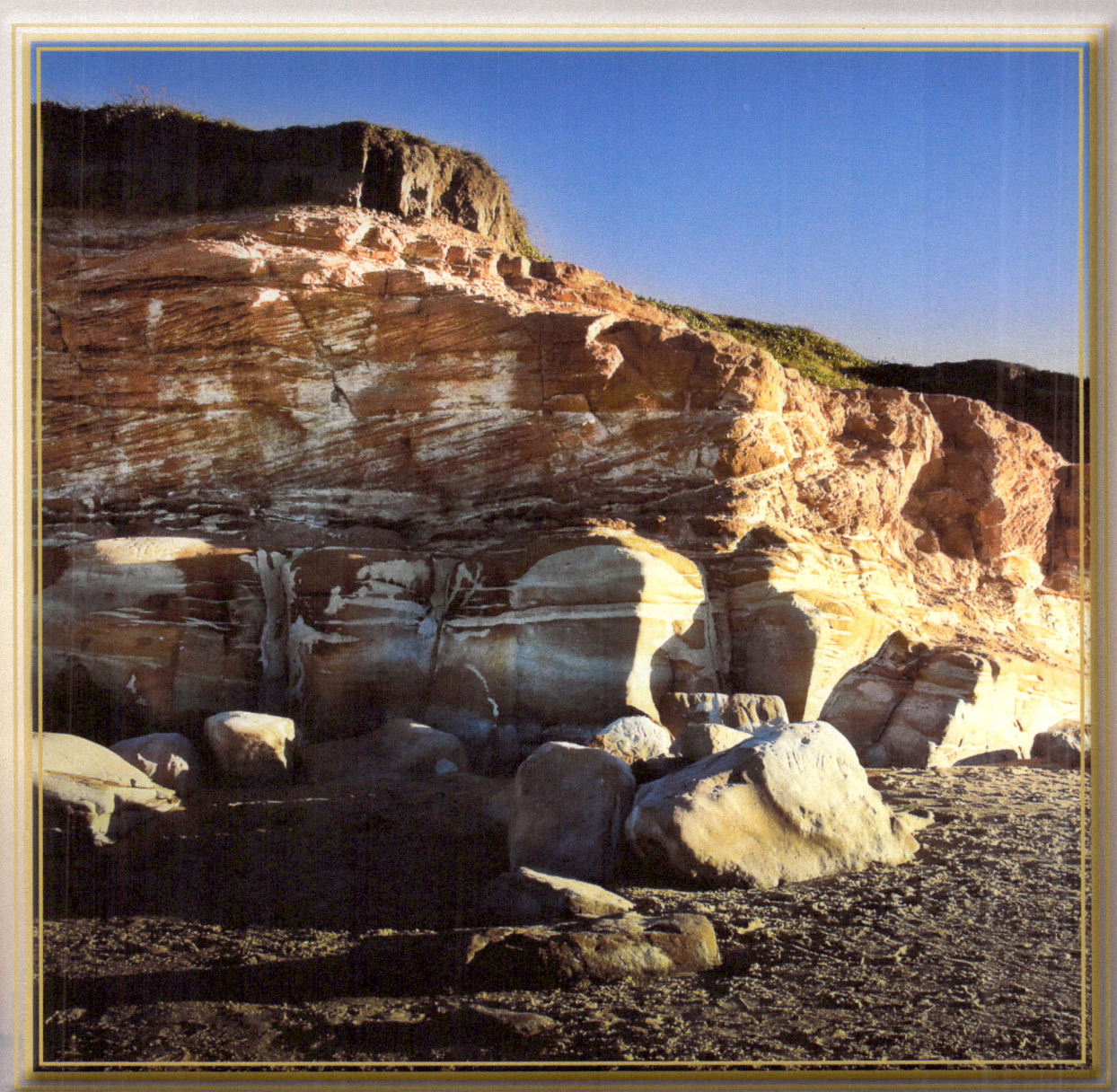

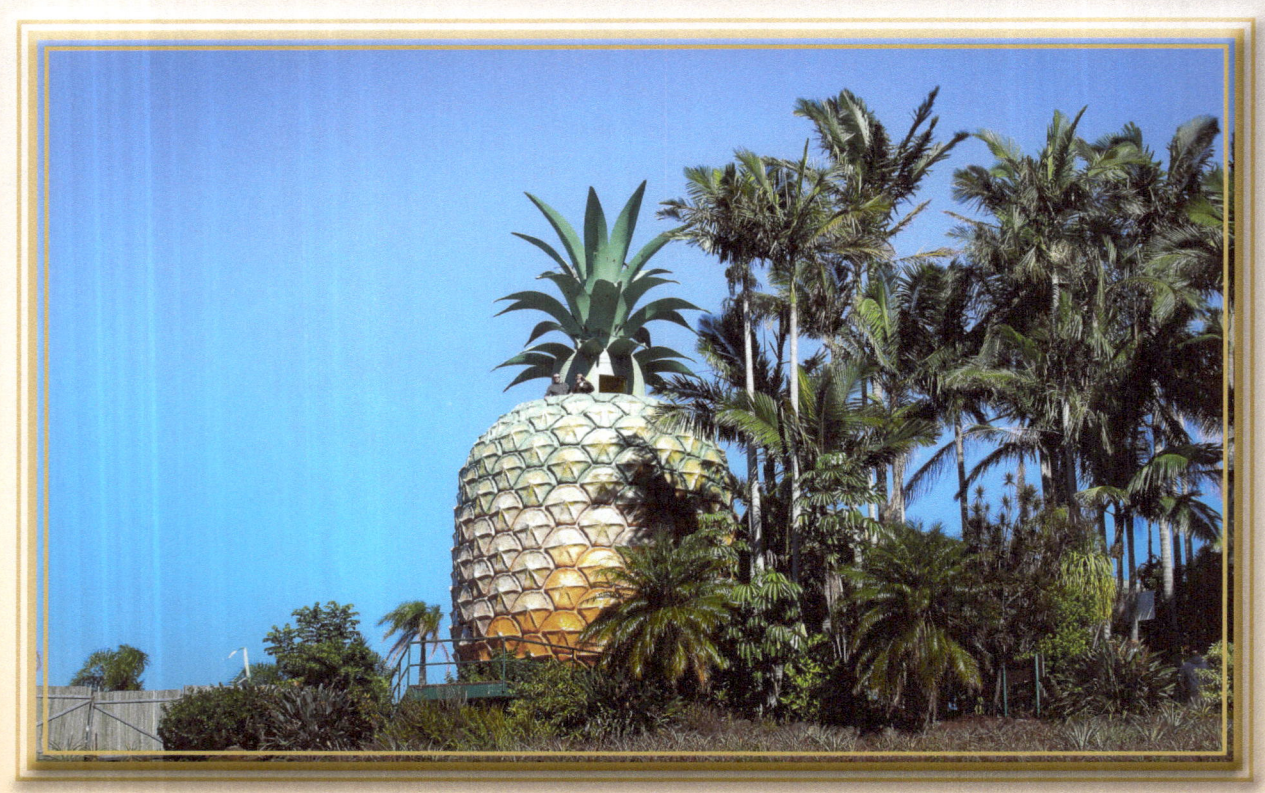

## The Big Pineapple - Woombye

The Big Pineapple is a heritage-listed tourist attraction on the Sunshine Coast in South East Queensland, Australia. It is 16 metres high and was originally opened on 15th August 1971.

It is situated on a 165 hectare site. The Big Pineapple features a small train ride that takes passengers on a tour of the plantation and lets them optionally disembark at a small zoo situated on the property.

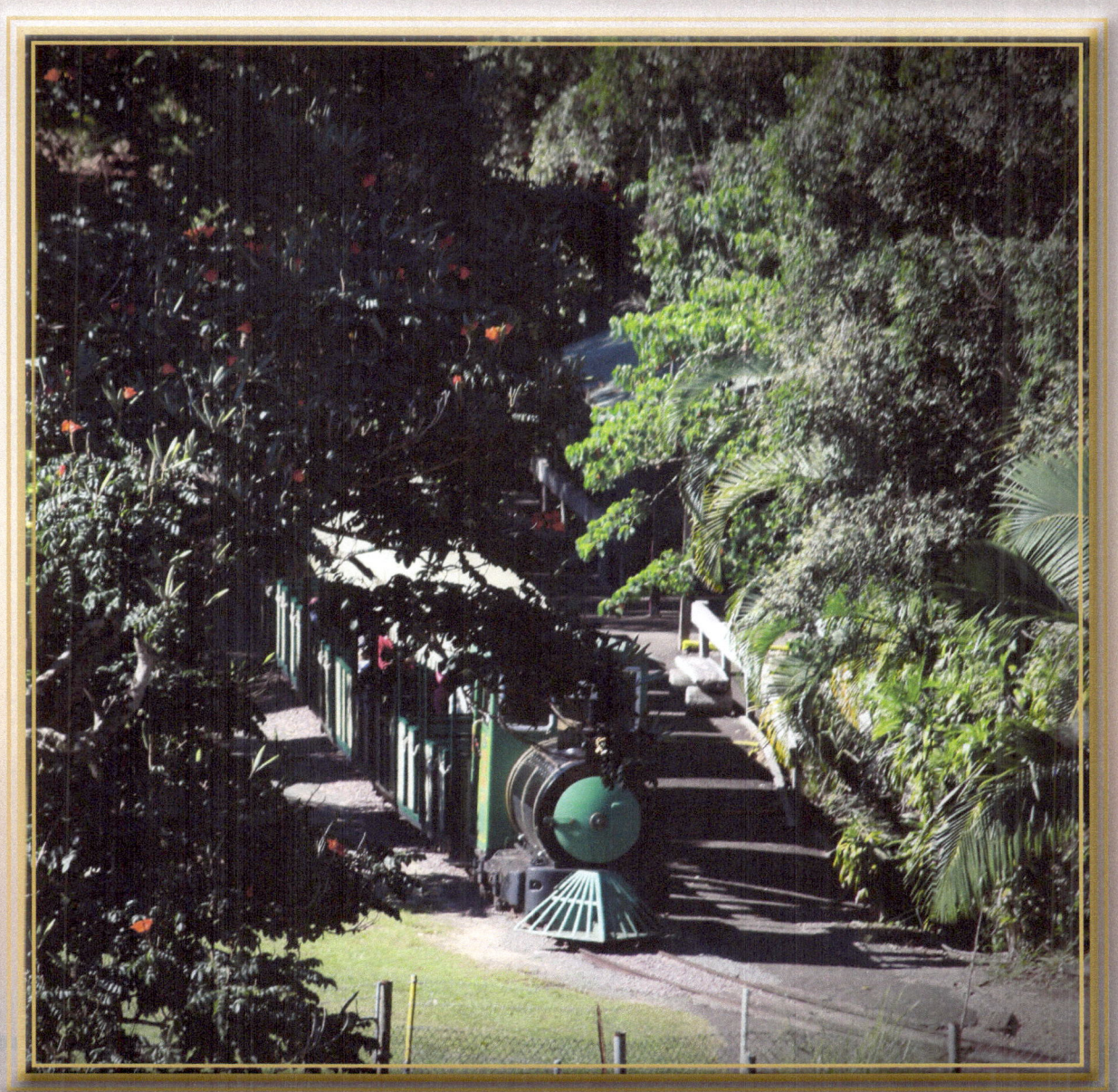

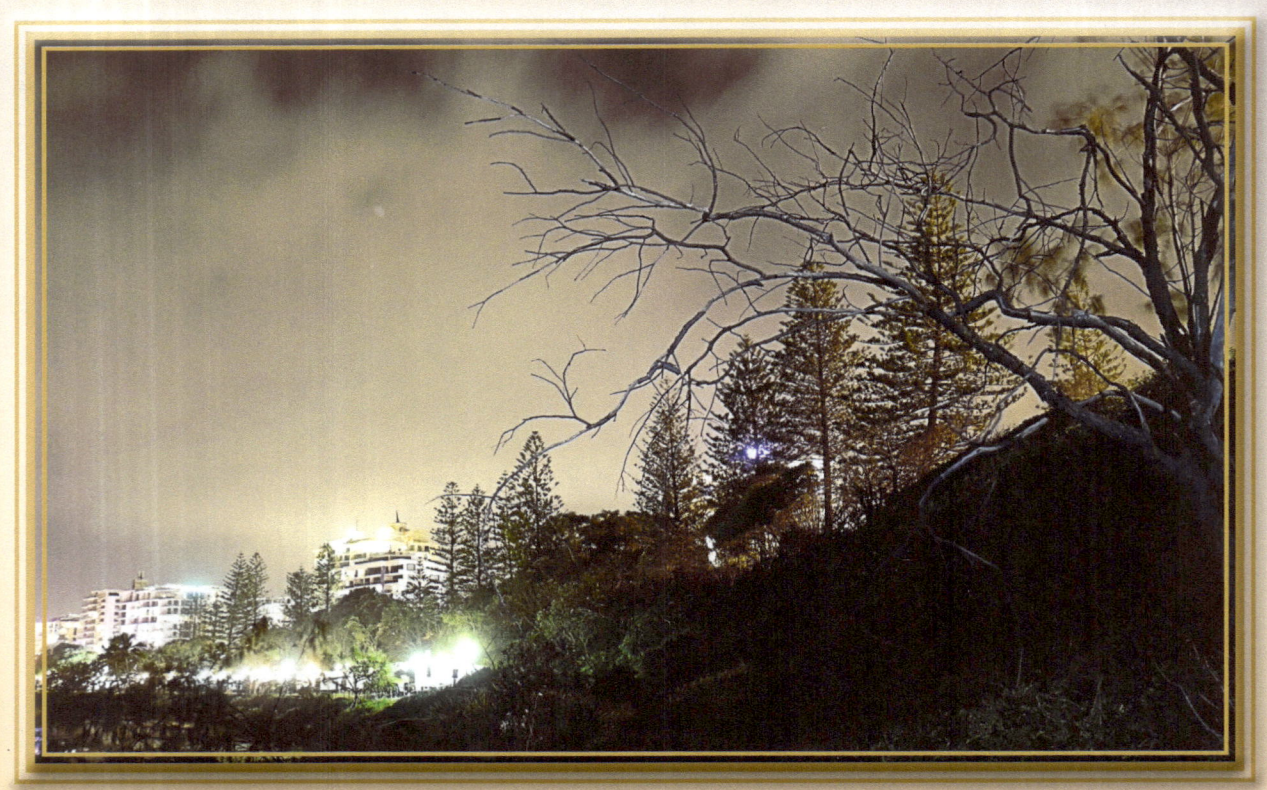

# Alexandra Headlands

Alexandra Headland is a suburb of the Sunshine Coast Region, Queensland, Australia, located in the Maroochydore urban centre between Maroochydore CBD and Mooloolaba. The suburb consists of several restaurants, a bowling alley, resorts and the shortest beach in the Maroochy district.

The headland was once known as Potts Point, named after overseer John Potts employed by William Pettigrew who lived on the land from the years 1880 to 1890.

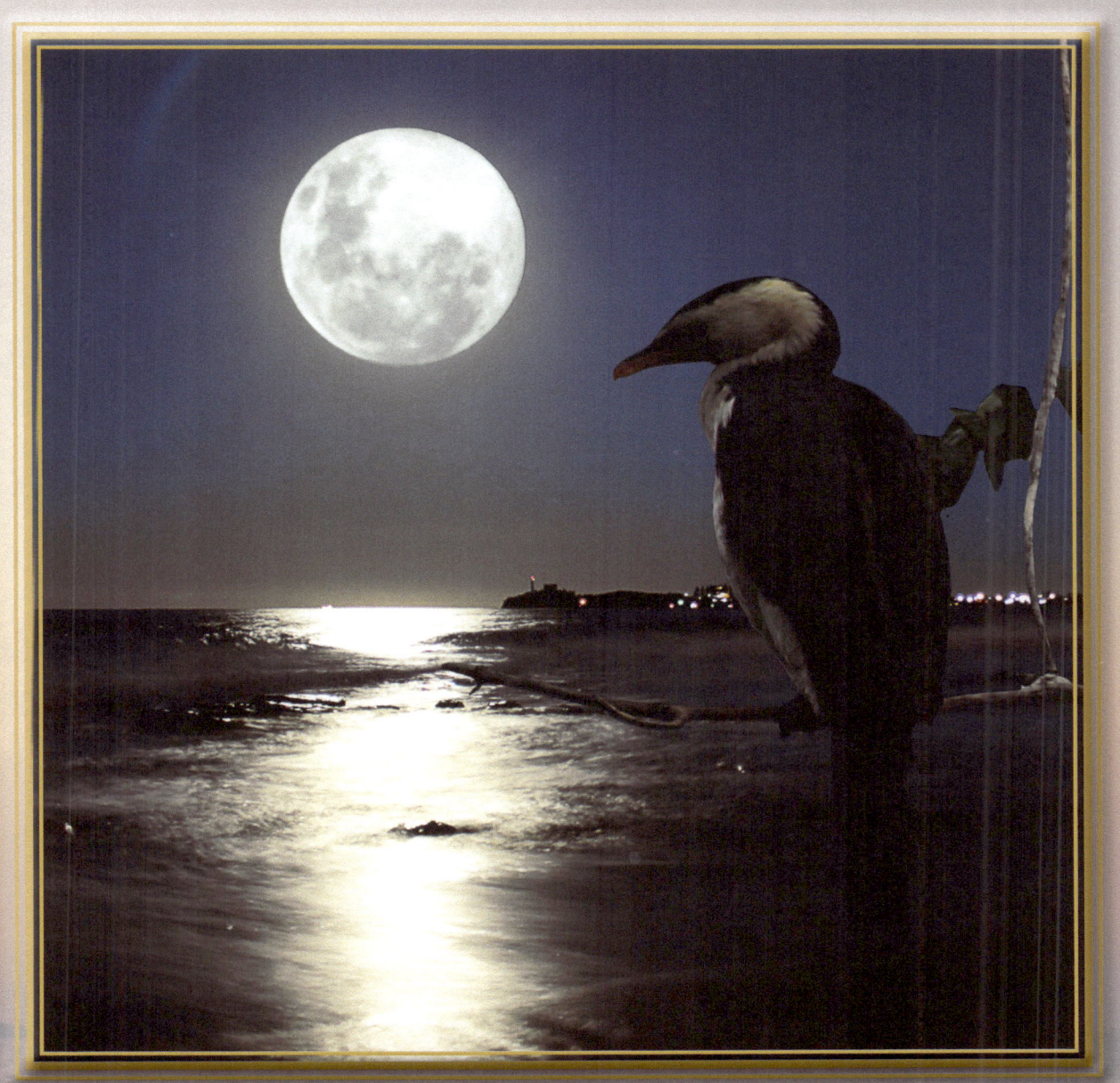

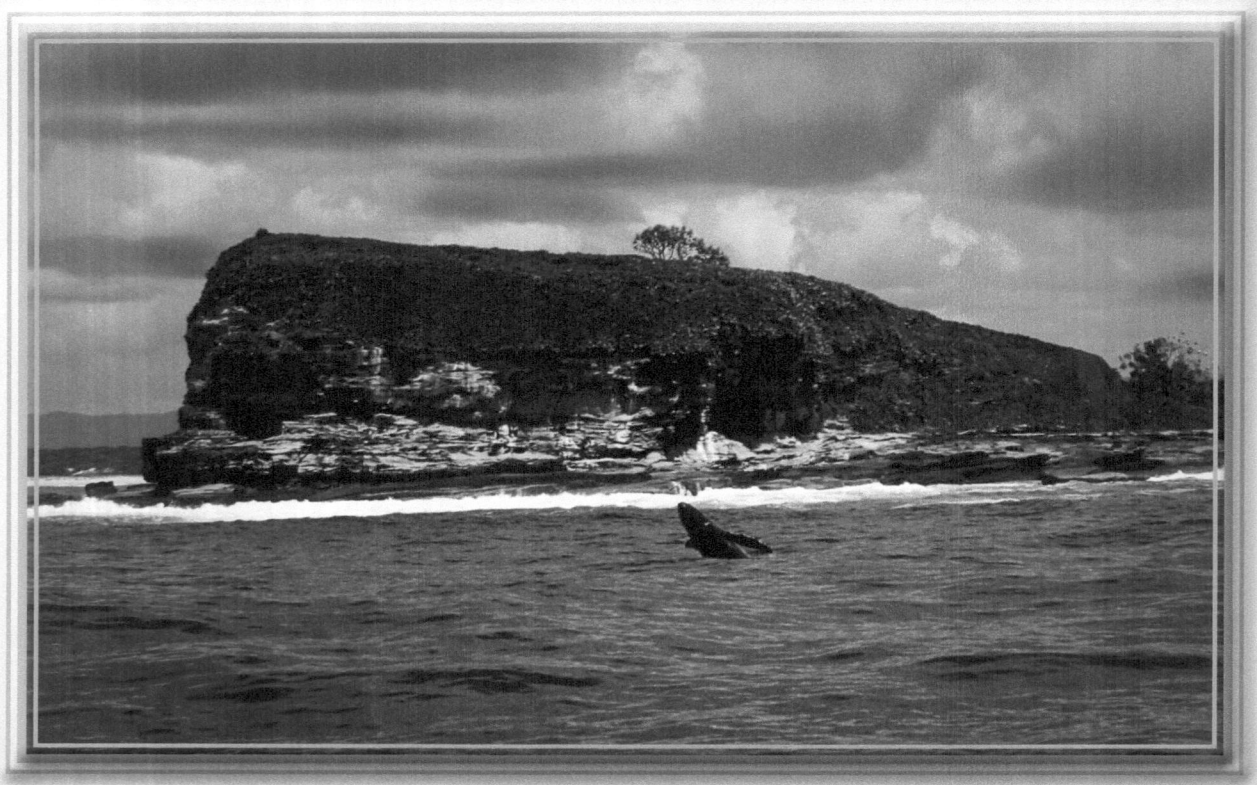

## Old Woman Island

Old Woman Island (also referred to as Mudjimba Island) is located about one kilometre off the coast of Mudjimba and can be clearly seen for miles up and down the coastline.

Aboriginal legends abound about the Island. One has it that the Island was the result of an epic battle between two men, Coolum and Ninderry, and a woman called Maroochy. The end result was that Coolum's head was knocked off and ended up in the ocean, creating Mudjimba Island. Mount Coolum, seven kilometres to the north, is now flat topped due to the lack of a head!

Sourse: www.sunshinecoast-australia.com

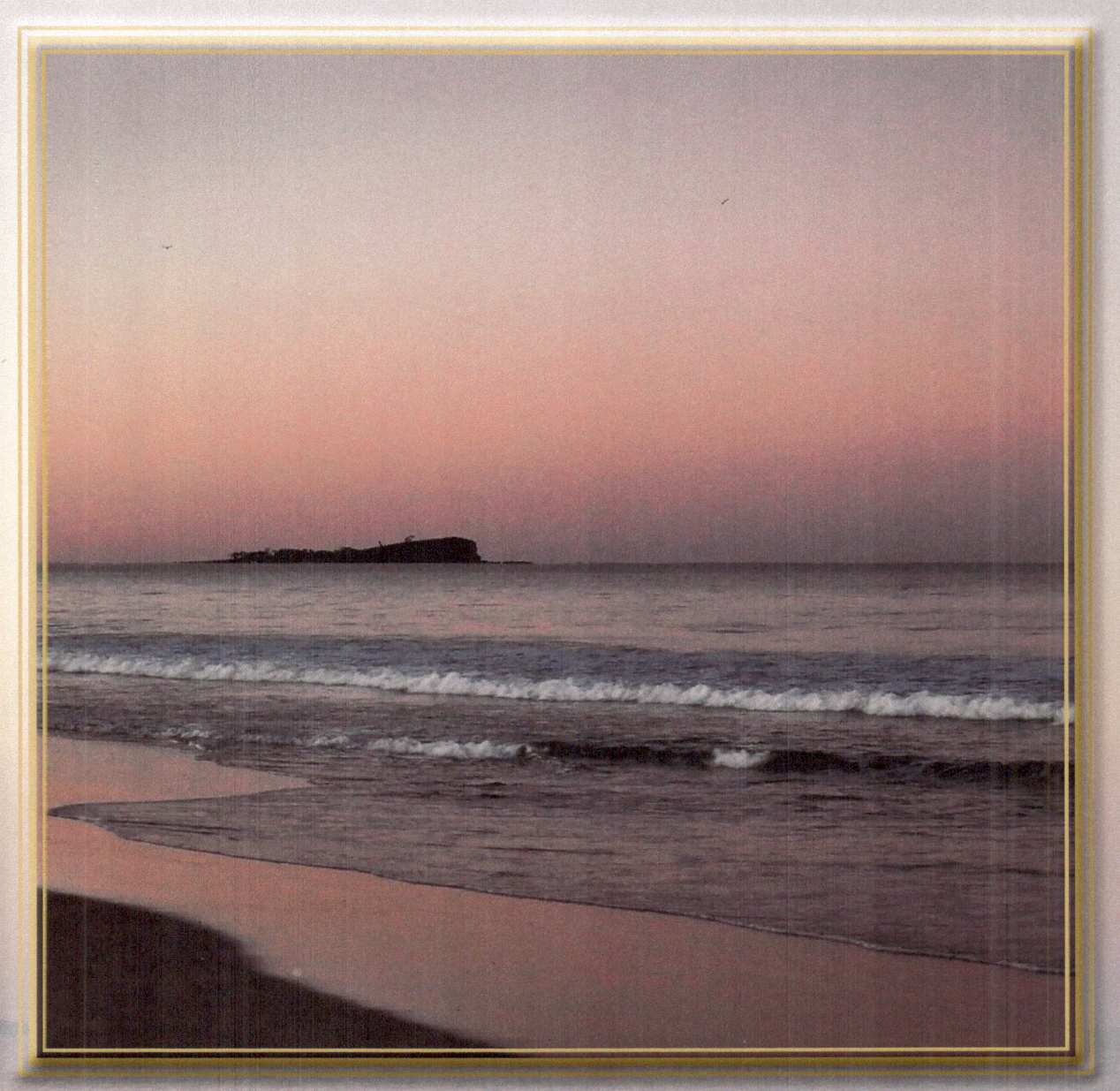

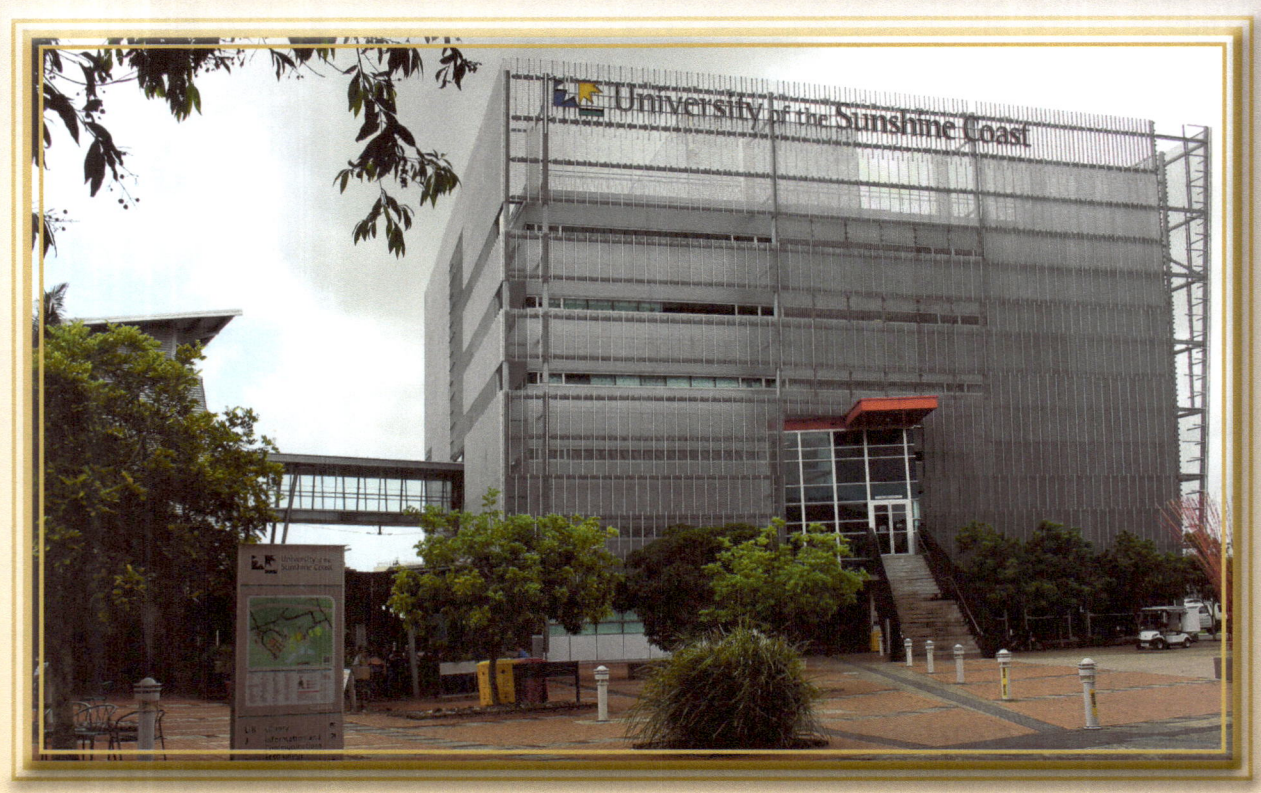

# University of the Sunshine Coast

The University of the Sunshine Coast (USC) is a public university based on the Sunshine Coast in Queensland, Australia. Having opened in 1996 as the Sunshine Coast University College with 524 students, it was renamed the University of the Sunshine Coast in 1999.

As at Semester 1 2015, the student body was 12,000. About 100 kilometres north of Brisbane, the campus is a 100-hectare flora and fauna reserve, adjoining the Mooloolah River National Park.

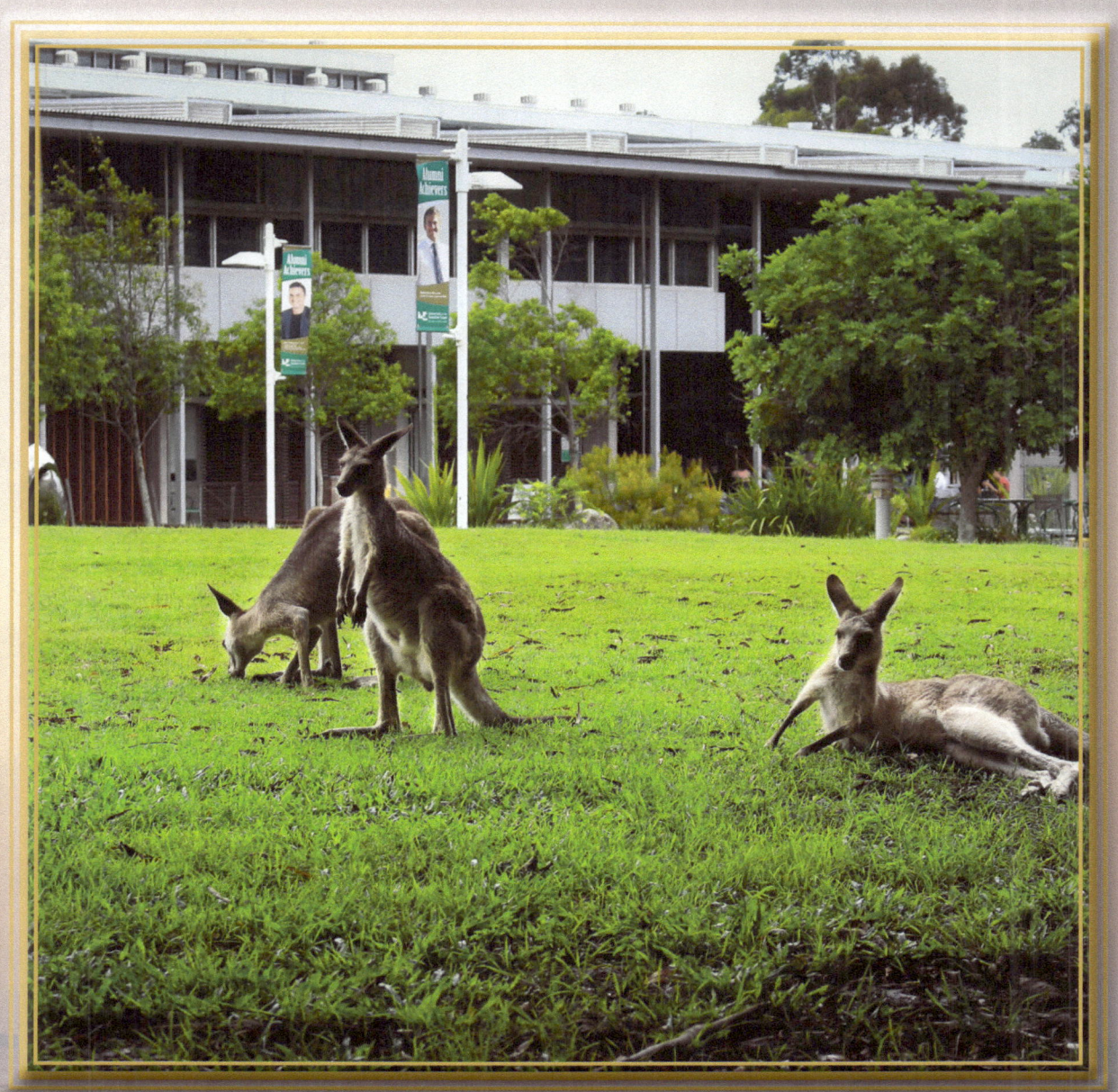

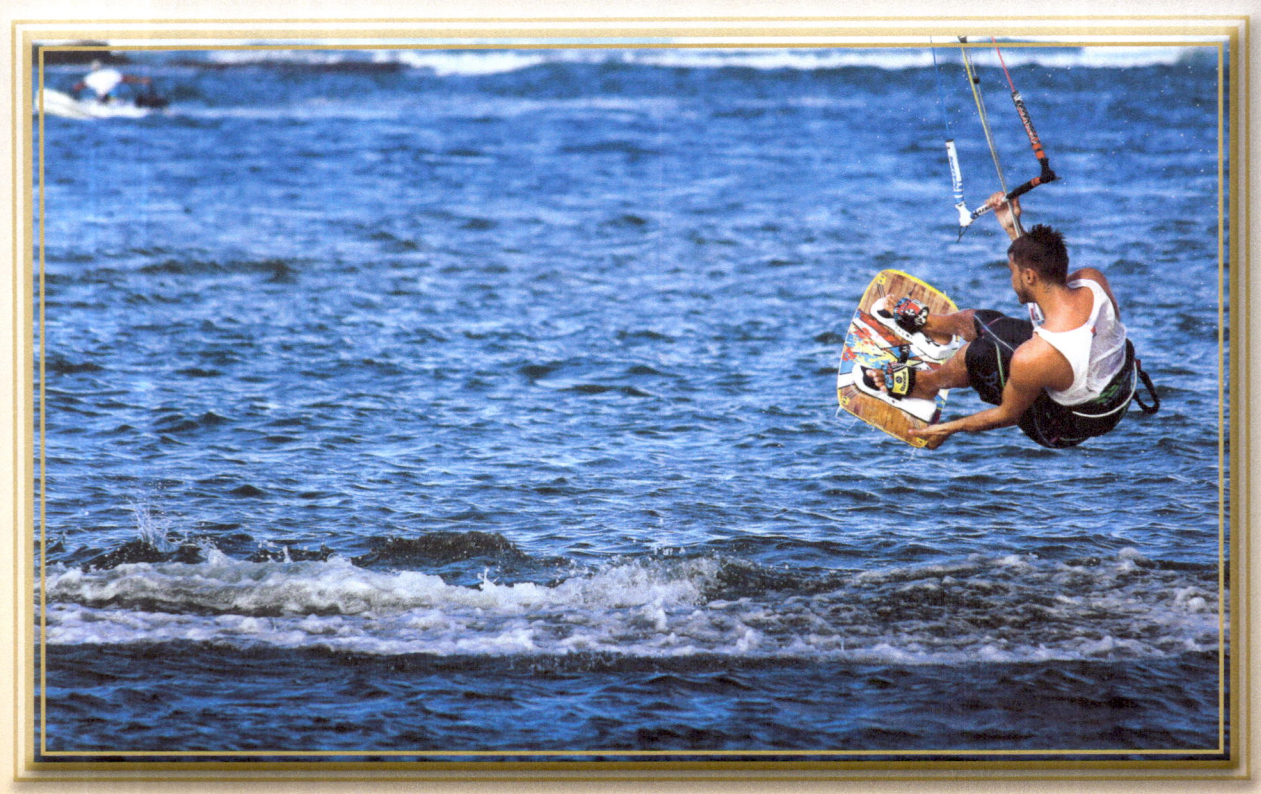

# Maroochy River Mouth

The Maroochy River is a river in South East Queensland, Australia.

The river rises from the eastern slopes of the Blackall Range and flows east through Eumundi, before entering the sea at Cotton Tree, Maroochydore.

The Maroochy River Mouth is very popular with kite surfers and other water sports.

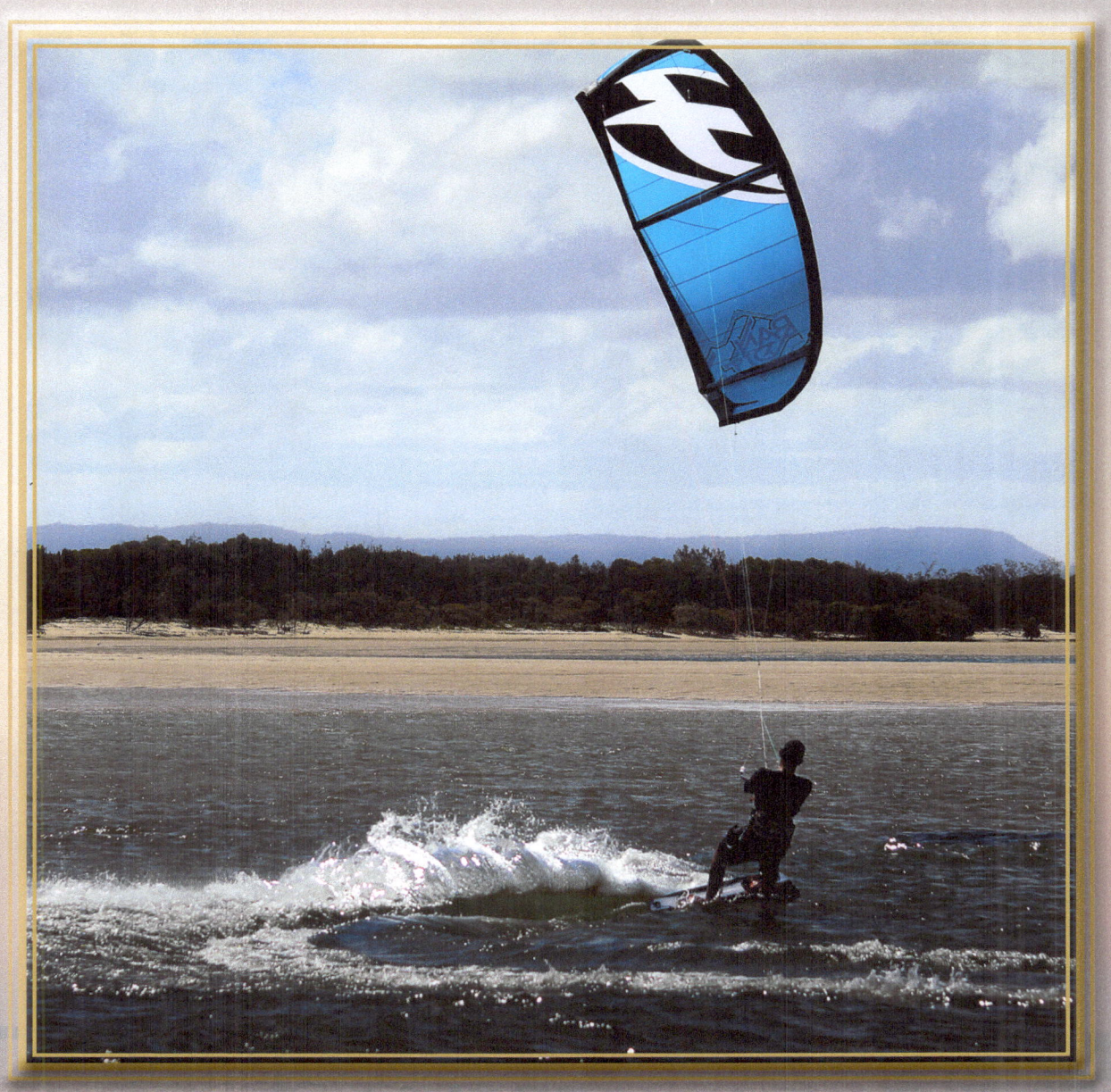

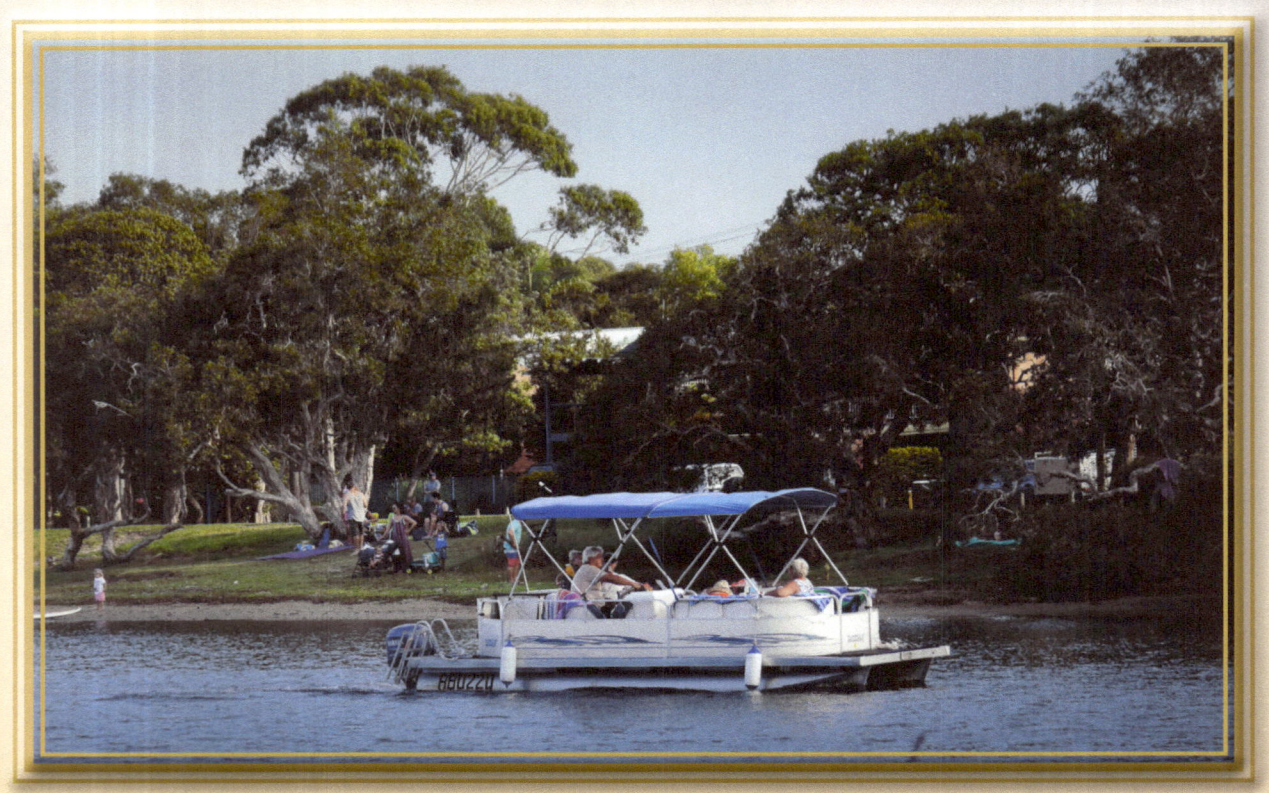

# Currimundi Lake

Currimundi Lake is a saltwater lake situated beside Currimundi Beach. The lake features in a children's book, "The Oobleegooblers of Lake Currimundi" by Kath Dewhurst, published in 1977, which is based on a local Aboriginal story.

Nicklin Way, the main road between Caloundra and Maroochydore, crosses Ahern Bridge over Currimundi Lake. The Ahern Bridge was named after John Ahern, a firefighter who saved many lives and won a bravery award.

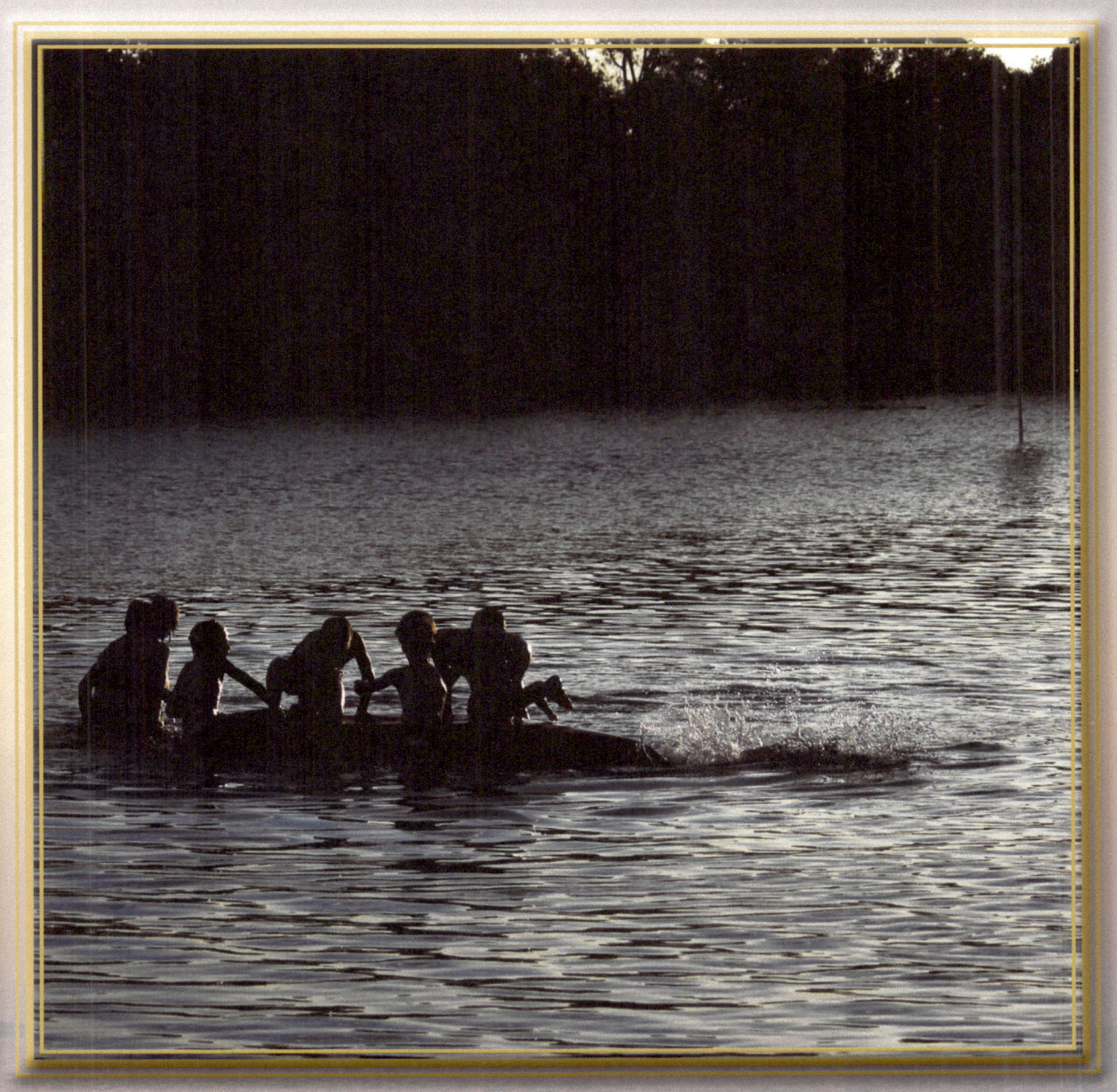

# Solé Paez, Australia
## BBus Marketing & Graphic Design

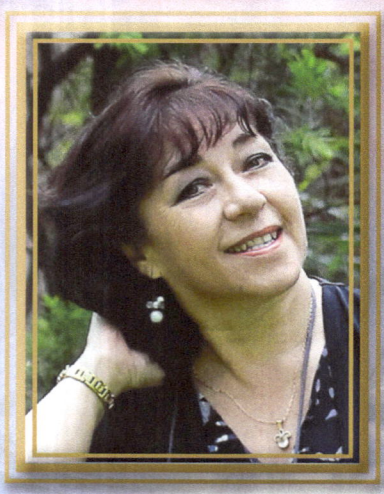

Solé was born in Chile and moved to Australia in 1983.

Mother of two, Solé's first love in the creative industry was drawing and painting.

In 1996, this natural talent motivated her to study Graphic Design at the University of the Sunshine Coast, QLD Australia.

Solé's second passion was always photography, making a more serious move into it in 2005 after winning the Maroochy Shire Council annual Photography Award.

Since then, photography has always been in her life, motivating her to manage a large group of photography enthusiasts.

These organised group photography sessions make it easier and safer for people to access areas that you otherwise would not go on your own with photography in mind.

Landscapes, flowers, butterflies, birds, astrophotography and interesting places are some of the many subjects Solé loves; thus this collection of images if the Sunshine Coast came to mind.

**E:** info@allmediaservices.com.au
PO Box 1099
Buderim - QLD 4556
Australia

www.ingramcontent.com/pod-product-compliance
Lightning Source LLC
Chambersburg PA
CBHW050904180526
45159CB00007B/2784